Population Education

Population Education

Raghunath Rao

AUTHORSPRESS

Publishers of Creative & Scholarly Books

Worldwide Circulation through Authorspress Global Network

First Published 2008

by

Authorspress

E-35/103, Jawahar Park
Laxmi Nagar, Delhi-110 092
e-mail: authorspress@yahoo.com

Population Education

ISBN 981-89012-50-2

Printed in India at Kensington Press

Preface

The vast population explosion of the 20th century has compelled many to evaluate the implications of this phenomenon, especially in a country like India, where its population has been a double-edged sword since the boom in the number of people. On the one hand, white the numbers ostensibly seem to resolve the issue of human resource, they have put under a great strain he resources of natural resources, jeopardising the growth and development of the nation. Education in this regard also comes into play in a big way, both in terms of the onerous task of educating such a large number of providing them with jobs, as well as employing it as a tool to curb the population growth.

This book, written to serve the needs of students pursing their Masters' in Education, focuses on the issue of population education. Population dynamics need to be under strict vigilance to maintain the vital balance between human numbers and resources, and education herein serves to be a crucial mode of control. The book undertaken a comprehensive and incisive analysis of education for the population, contextualising it within the Indian scenario, and the intermingled effects and process of this within the political, social, economic and cultural realism of the nation. Delving into the developmental strategy of the nation, it also explores the perceptions of the population phenomenon and its relationship with the development variables, which require a fresh look at education in terms of large numbers of people. In addition, it also takes a look at the content and methodology of population education paying close attention to such issues as population health, human rights, employment, basic social needs, etc.

It is hoped that the insight incorporated in the book proves informative for the readers.

Contents

CHAPTER 1

Introduction to Population Education

Population education, which emerged as an educational innovation in response to population problems only about four decades ago, is now being experimented in over a hundred countries of the world in non-too-uniform a manner. It has been introduced in the education systems of different countries as an important component of the multi-pronged strategy employed to help nations attain the goals of population stabilisation and sustainable development. Very few educational programmes have matched its pace of expansion and adopted such varied conceptual frameworks and strategies of curriculum transaction. Perhaps no other educational concept has experienced such frequent changes in its framework and been subjected to so many misunderstandings as the concept of population education. This has been so because of not only the nature of the context in which it emerged but also it's newness and its complex characteristics.

1.1. Population and Development

The concept of population education emerged in the context of population and development - the two most pressing issues before humankind today. Both are closely interrelated and both encompass a number of complex factors. Viewed as an epiphenomenon of the process of development, population issues have aroused widespread concern among almost all the members of the comity of nations. There have been undaunted endeavours to accelerate the pace of socioeconomic development through the instrumentalities of science and technology and to secure distributive justice for the people through different institutional mechanisms. But those are confronted with some basic population related questions of how many people are going to inhabit the earth, how they are to be supported and enabled to make their contributions to development efforts, what they are going to bequeath to posterity and how long they are going to be sustained by the natural and human resource base. The rapid population growth and the concomitant problems of poverty, lack of adequate health and educational facilities, malnutrition, non-fulfilment of even the basic needs of a vast majority of the populace, paucity of employment opportunities, dwindling natural resources and consequent environmental degradation constitute critical dimensions of the present population and development phenomena. It is also pertinent to note that the population phenomenon today embraces issues beyond development. While the size, growth, composition and distribution of population have a close bearing on socioeconomic development, the population related issues also bring forth concerns for the "carrying capacity" of biological and ecological system and the future of mankind.

1.1.1. Need for Population Education

It has been gradually realised that since the interrelationship between population and development is highly complex and population problems are multidimensional, it will not yield to any single solution. It is basically related to the developmental needs of a nation and its people. Demographic trends influence, and are influenced by, the level of development and the quality of life of the people. The population situation of any nation largely depends on the demographic behaviour of its people. Changes in the demographic profile of a nation depend largely on attitudes and behaviours of individuals in respect of population and development issues. The demographic behaviour is to a great extent informed by population socialisation, a process by which people acquire norms, values, attitudes and belief systems in respect of population related issues and which is embedded within the larger complexes of social practices reflecting the society's internal logical system. This process is greatly influenced by education, which enables the individual to know the phenomenon of population change and its consequences. It is commonly observed in many countries that the knowledge of the simple facts of population change, let alone the complex interrelationships with other parameters, is very low even among educated people. It is precisely because of these complexities that population education has emerged as an integral part of the multi-pronged strategy employed to solve contemporary population problems that face the nations.

1.1.2. Emergence of Population Education

The idea that population education can play a potential role in addressing population problems, was first mooted in Sweden in 1935. The Population Commission of Sweden, which expressed its concern on the declining rates of birth in that country, recommended a comprehensive and truly vigorous educational campaign to clarify population related issues aimed at influencing the fertility behaviour of individuals. A similar view was expressed in the United States during 1937-38. Since the birth rate continued to decline and population seemed to be dwindling, it was suggested that population studies be included as a content area in the school curriculum. However, nothing noteworthy happened during the next two decades.

It was in the 1960s that the matter was seriously reconsidered in the United States. Warren S. Thompson and Philip M. Hauser published papers in march 1962 issue of Teachers College Record, Columbia University reiterating the inclusion of population content in the school curriculum. Interestingly, they made such recommendations in a completely different context, as the perception of population problem had changed during 1960s and the concern had shifted from decline in growth rate to rapid population growth in both the industrialised and developing worlds. In the fifties and sixties, therefore, efforts were initiated in a number of countries to arrest population growth; and motivational activities for adults provided information about the consequences of high birth rate. The information, education and communication "IEC" or information education and motivation "IEM" strategy was employed in family planning programmes to achieve the desired objectives. However, in the developing world the "IEC" activities of family planning programmes were not always as successful as had been expected. It was in this context that the potential of education was realised in order to overcome deeply entrenched traditional learning that influenced demographic behaviour of the people. The school education, in particular, was considered effective for achieving this objective. However, the nomenclature of population education was given to this educational innovation at a later date. Sloan Wayland was the first to use the term "population education".

The first national endeavour to evolve and concretise the concept of population education was made in India in 1969 and then in the

Philippines and the Republic of Korea in 1970. The Workshop on Population and Family Education sponsored by the UNESCO Regional Office for Education in Asia held in September 1970 at Bangkok, was a land-mark in the history of population education. It not only facilitated the identification of objectives of population education, the selection of suitable contents and the consideration of strategies for introduction of population education into formal and non-formal education systems but also resulted in the launching of national population education programmes by many countries in Asia. Similar activities were initiated by UNESCO Regional Offices in Santiago (Latin America and Caribbean) and Dakar (Africa South of the Sahara). The United Nations Population Fund (UNFPA), previously known as United Nations Fund for Population Activities, played a vital role in appreciating the potential of population education and providing funds for national programmes from the late sixties onwards.

Population education emerged as an educational innovation during 1970s and various countries initiated activities to introduce it into their ongoing education systems. The recommendations of the World Population Plan of Action adopted at the 1974 World Population Conference held in Bucharest, also encouraged nations to adopt the strategy of population education. The Plan of Action recommended that "the Governments should consider making provision, in both the formal and non-formal educational programmes, for informing their people on the consequences of existing or alternative fertility behaviour for the well-being of the family, for the educational and psychological development of children and for the general welfare of society, so that an informed and responsible attitude to marriage and reproduction will be promoted".

In India, the Family Planning Association for the first time sent a Memorandum to the State Government of Maharashtra in 1968 recommending that education in population dynamics should be made a part of school curriculum. However, the idea of population education was crystallised in the National Seminar on Population Education organised in Bombay in August 1969. It recommended that population education should be introduced into curriculum of schools and colleges. The Seminar made an attempt to define population education in the context of Indian situation, but more importantly, expressed the national consensus for introducing this educational innovation in the education system of the country.

1.1.3. Other Concepts

In the initial phase of its evolution, there were several misconceptions regarding population education, and some of those still continue to affect its proper understanding. Population education was popularly equated with family planning or family planning education, primarily because of its emergence in close association with the "IEC" or "IEM" activities of the family planning programmes. It was also regarded as a euphemism for sex education and family life education, as in some countries the concerned programmes approached population issues in terms of sexuality.

Population education was also equated with population studies, and even now both the terms are sometimes used interchangeably, because the core of the knowledge base of population education, (the basic core content upon which the population education curriculum is developed), contained the elements of population studies. While population education is none of these "educations" in the true sense, it draws contents from all those educational areas the objectives of which are mutually supportive. It is necessary, therefore, to discuss the nature and objectives of certain related areas, as it may help in proper understanding of the distinction and complementarity between population education and them.

1.1.4. Family Planning

In many countries population programmes were initiated as family planning programmes which had a special "IEC" or "IEM" component. This component came to be popularly known also as family planning education. In some countries this campaign was launched in a very narrow sense aimed at creating awareness about controlling birth by using contraceptives. It helped in the supply and use of contraceptives to eligible couples. But over the years family planning also has adopted a broad orientation. It is now increasingly being regarded more than an intervention to promote the use of contraception. It is a means of caring for the health of mother and child, enhancing the quality of families by regulating and spacing child birth, raising the age at marriage and improving the position of girls and women, helping sub-fertile couples to beget children and providing counselling for parents and potential parents.

Despite these changes, the family planning education continues to address itself primarily to adults and youth, and its approach also remains predominantly prescriptive, explaining the oversimplified dogmatism of assertions like "small family is a happy family". Population education shares all the content of the family planning education and also focuses on its objectives. But the scheme of contents of population education is broader and its specific objectives are more varied than those of the family planning education. Both have basic differences in their approach. Population education does not follow prescriptive and didactic approaches. Whereas family planning education aims at conveying specific messages of family size and quality of life issues, population education focuses on influencing attitude and behaviour of individuals and developing basic thinking and decision-making skills in them.

1.1.5. Sex Education

Sex Education is an educational programme designed to provide learners with adequate and accurate knowledge about human sexuality in its biological, psychological, socio-cultural and moral dimensions. It largely, though not exclusively, focuses on the individual self-awareness, personal relationships, human sexual development, reproduction and sexual behaviour. It also covers the anatomy and physiology of reproductive systems, physical, emotional and psychological changes during puberty and conception, pregnancy, and birth. It deals with sexual behaviour, sex roles and sexually transmitted diseases. Whereas population education deals with many of these contents, it focuses on their interrelationships with population issues and also on population processes other than fertility.

1.1.6. Family Life Education

Closely related to sex education, the family life education is an educational process designed to assist young people in their physical, social, emotional and moral development, as they prepare themselves for adulthood, marriage and parenthood. It deals with issues like ageing as well as social relationships in the sociocultural context of family and society. It provides an opportunity to the learners to study family relationships and peer relationships. It does not simply deal with physiology and anatomy of reproduction and human sexuality.

While population education includes these concerns in its scheme of content, it also covers many other issues that are beyond the scope of the family life education.

1.2. Population Studies

Population studies is the body of knowledge, concepts and theories, which describe and attempt at explaining the dynamics of human populations and their relationships with social, cultural, economic, political and biological environments. It focuses on population issues related to the demographic processes of fertility, mortality and migration. It also covers components such as population size, age and sex composition, its spatial distribution and socioeconomic characteristics. Population studies as a general body of knowledge, therefore, has made substantial contribution to the knowledge base of population education. During the initial years of the evolution of population education it was thought to be the be-all and end-all of population education, and the curriculum framers were expected to perform the simple task of including and hierarchically arranging the facts, theories and concepts of population studies into the scheme of content of population education. But over the years, the conceptual framework of population education has broadened to incorporate those components which do not belong to population studies but to other disciplines and professional fields, such as life sciences, medical sciences, social sciences, pedagogy, psychology and so on. Moreover, population related attitudes, behaviour and decisions, rather than the internal logic of population studies are characteristically the major concerns of population education.

1.3. Conclusion

Population education differs from all the areas delineated above in that its need arose under special historical circumstances and some typical contemporary issues. Family planning education was initiated with a view to conveying specific messages focussed on the need to control population growth. Sex education originally developed in response to the concern for changing sexual mores and increasing incidence of deviant sexual behaviour, venereal diseases and out of wedlock pregnancies. Family life education grew out of a recognition of the growing evidence of family instability and disintegration. Population studies evolved, not as a separate discipline but as an interdisciplinary body of knowledge by bringing together facts, theories and concepts based on the research studies conducted by the specialists of different disciplines and professional fields for explaining various facets of population phenomenon. Population education emerged as an educational response to the concern for population problems emanating from the changing inter-relationship between population and development.

It is primarily because of the context in which it emerged that population education, by its very nature, has been treated as a culture and region specific concept. Its definition in one country or region differs from that in the other. The numerosity of definitions is also the result of the constant changes being effected in the concept by including new areas of concern based on the experiences of international regional and national experimentation. Moreover, the definitions have been construed in various ways. Population education has been defined by describing the nature of activity or by stating objectives or contents or by spelling out behavioural outcomes. However, not all the definitions are actually different from one another; there is a substantial commonality among them with certain differences in the emphasis on some aspect or the other.

Population education is broadly defined as an educational intervention aimed at helping individuals in understanding the interrelationship between population and development, in appreciating the determinants and consequences of population processes and changes, in assessing the possible actions that they and their respective families and communities can take to modify these processes and in carrying out selected actions. It is a part of total social learning process and based on the premise that an educational intervention which helps the learners define problems and search for solutions will have greater impact than the prescriptive programme that employs only assertions.

References

Caldwell, J. C., "Mass education as a determinant of the timing of fertility decline", *Population and Development Review*, New York(June), 1980.

Cruz Leonardo de la, *Population education: Nature, goal and role,* Bangkok: UNESCO, 1978.

Hutabarat, Sans S., et al., *Population education in Indonesia,* Jakarta: National Family Planning Coordination Board, 1979.

Jacobson, Willard J., *Population education: A knowledge base,* New York: Teachers College, Columbia University, 1979.

NCERT, *Population education; A draft syllabus, (Mimeograph)*, New Delhi, NCERT, 1971.

NCERT, *Minimum essential contents of population education, (Mimeograph)*, New Delhi: NCERT, 1987.

NCERT, *National seminar on population education,* New Delhi: NCERT, 1969.

O.J., *Population education, International encyclopedia of population,* Volume One, New York: the Free Press, 1984.

Sharma, R.C., *Population resources, environment and quality of life,* Delhi: Dhanpat Rai & Sons, 1988.

Sheshadri, C. and J.L. Pandey, *Population education: A national source book*, New Delhi: NCERT, 1991.

UNESCO, "Population education: A contemporary concern", *ISCOMPE Education Studies Documents* No. 28, Paris: UNESCO, 1978.

UNFPA, "Programme of action", *adopted at the International Conference on Population and Development*, Cairo, New York: UNFPA, 5-13 September 1994.

Valkonen, T., "Differentials and trends in life expectancy by gender and occupational class: measurement and explanations", *Paper presented at the seminar on health and other welfare differences between population groups*, Helsinki, 13 and 14 March 2000.

Wellings, Kaye., Teenage Sexual and Reproductive Behavior in Developed Countries: Country Report for Great Britain, *Occasional Report*, No. 6. New York and Washington, 2000.

Winkleby, M. A., and others, "Socioeconomic status and health: how education, income and occupation contribute to risk factors for cardiovascular disease", *American Journal of Public Health*, Washington, D.C.

World Bank, "Priorities and Strategies for Education", *A World Bank Review*, Washington, D.C.: World Bank, 1995.

CHAPTER 2

Population Education in India

2.1. Introduction

Since its inception the conceptual framework of population education has been changing quite frequently because of the changes in the perception of population phenomenon and its relationships with development variables. Every time when there was a change in the perception pattern of population issues, a need was felt to reconceptualise population education. Although the changes that have occurred in the conceptual framework of population education in different countries over the years have reflected the context-specific variations, there has been an overarching commonness in them. And hence, the understanding of the process of evolution of the concept of sometimes erroneously, population education in one country such as India will provide adequate insight into its evolution throughout the world.

2.1.1. Conceptualisation of Population Education

The first attempt to conceptualise population education in India was made during late 1960s. The National Seminar on Population Education held in August 1969 made the following recommendations to define the concept:

i) The objective of population education should be to enable the students to understand that family size is controllable, that population limitation can facilitate the development of a higher quality of life. It should also enable the students to appreciate the fact that for preserving the health and welfare of the members of the family, ensuring economic stability to the family. The Indian family of today should be small with only two or three children.

ii) "Students at all levels have a right to accurate information about the effect of changes in family size and in national population on the individual, the family and the nation so that this body of knowledge is utilised to control family size and national population

iii) "Population should not be treated merely as a quantitative phenomenon. It is the quality of the population that is most relevant both as a factor of growth and an end product of growth.

Population education is an educational intervention to make the target groups aware of the multi-faceted population phenomenon so that it leads them eventually to take rational decisions concerning population matters. The Syllabus contained a scheme of content which was developed by drawing contents from the six major content areas - population growth, population and economic development, population and social development, population health and nutrition, population, biological factors and family life and ecological considerations and population. Population education thus was treated as a demography-laden concept, predominantly as education in demography and population studies.

Evaluation studies on various facets of the implementation of the National Population Education Project identified significant gaps in the integration of elements of population education in content and process of school education. It was realised that since population education had been treated as a demography-laden concept, its ambitious conceptual framework, with excessive elements of population dynamics, had hindered the process of effective integration of its elements into the school curriculum.

The National Policy on Education 1986 which reflected the magnitude of the major causes and consequences of rapid population growth also specified "promotion of observance of small family norm" as one of the core curricular areas to be reflected in the national system of education. It provided an appropriate context to reconceptualise population education. Moreover, nearly half of the ten core curricular areas identified by the policy document such as equality of sexes, protection of environment, removal of social barriers, and inculcation of scientific temper were considered critical for realising population education objectives.

During the process of revision of the conceptual framework of population education in India, six major themes: family size and family welfare, delayed marriage, responsible parenthood, population change and resource development, population related values and beliefs, and status of women were identified. The scheme of content was prepared by drawing contents relating to these major themes from the following six content areas: economic development, social development, environment and resources, family life, health and nutrition, and demographic implications. The reconceptualised framework also emphasised the strategy of integrating maximum contents at minimum points in order to provide comprehensive treatment to contents to make the integration of population education elements in the textbooks more effective. The new conceptual framework defined population education as an education in the interrelationships among population, development, resources, environment and quality of life.

2.1.2. Re-conceptualisation

All concepts having an interactive relationship with social environment require reconsideration particularly after a perceptible change takes place in the context in which they were formulated. Sometimes, it is the odd fate of a concept to have too successful a rein. After it secures scientific acceptance, it may become so popular and fashionable that it is applied indiscriminately, leading to the dilution of its essential characteristics, generating a need to resuscitate it. The concept of population education has also undergone such a process.

The need to reorient the conceptual framework of population education was reflected in the Istanbul Declaration and the Plan of Action adopted by the International Conference on Population Education and Development, 1993, which brought forth the limitations of the existing concept and recommended the inclusion of a number of emerging concerns in it. But the reconceptualisation of population education was necessitated by the latest and most striking development of a global consensus on population and development. In course of Population Debate since Malthus initiated it, population phenomenon has been analysed in view of perceptions of its interrelationships with other variables of development and social environment. The present perceptions of the patterns of these interrelationships reflected in the Programme of Action (POA) adopted by the International Conference on Population and Development, held in Cairo inl994, made it an imperative requirement for planned interventions addressed to population phenomenon to reorient, revitalise and rejuvenate themselves to realise the vision of the new paradigm of population and development.

The ICPD Programme of Action has effected what is being described as "Paradigm Shift" from number to conditions for population stabilisation. It is considered essential now to focus on the individual needs instead of demographic targets and to integrate population concerns into development strategies rather than pursuing and providing sustenance to population control approach. Moreover, the ICPD for the first time has explicated two distinct roles of education: (a) education as a key factor in population stabilisation; and (b) education as a means to promote greater responsibility and awareness of the interrelationships between population and sustainable development. The need to shift from purely demographic or population control approach to a broader sustainable development approach has been advocated in other international conferences also.

2.1.3. National Population Education Project

The Population Education Framework even after the first reconceptualisation did not include elements relating to the process of growing up and HIV/AIDS, as these elements had been regarded very sensitive. But without these elements the Population Education Framework remained incomplete. In view of the problems that adolescents have been confronting for lack of authentic knowledge about the process of growing up from childhood to adulthood and the recently realised urgency to impart HIV/AIDS education, it was felt that the Population Education Framework must incorporate all the elements that had been considered crucial for attaining the objectives of population education.

Moreover, the Framework of Population Education being primarily influenced by the IEC approach had not been in consonance with the existing school curriculum framework, and hence the gaps in effective integration. Population education tended to be didactic making efforts to convey messages. But the existing school framework is open-ended and is considered a process during which messages are caught. Population education, therefore, needed to be reconceptualised as an educational endeavour that would make the learners aware of all possible dimensions of population - development interrelationships, promoting a general approach of supporting and empowering learners to take rational decisions regarding population and development issues; and also making them aware of the social consequences of their individual decisions. Accordingly, the population education framework was once again reconceptualised. It makes an attempt to focus on all possible variables that interact with population and development phenomena and to bring the concept of population education in tune with the existing school curriculum.

2.1.4. Reconceptualised Framework

2.1.4.1. Definition of population education

The reconceptualised framework provides a broader definition to the concept of population education, which mirrors the basic tenets of the ICPD Programme of Action. Population Education is defined as an educational process which develops among learners an understanding of interrelationships between population and development, causes and consequences of population change, and the criticality of the conditions for population stabilisation. It inculcates in them rational attitude and responsible behaviour towards population and development issues, so that they may make informed decisions.

Population education does not have its own content; it draws contents from the existing disciplines and attempts at providing the needed focus to those contents. Only such contents are borrowed from concerned disciplines as have the potential to help this educational intervention attain its objectives. The scheme of content of the Reconceptualised Framework, therefore, contains those contents that have been selected from the existing disciplines and that meet the requirements reflected in the ICPD Programme of Action. These contents have been placed under the six basic themes in the following manner.

2.1.5. Integration Strategy

Population education has been accepted as a critical curricular area and not as a separate subject, and hence efforts have been made to integrate its elements in the entire content and process of school education and teacher education. Since population education draws its contents from the existing disciplines of social sciences and sciences, it has been found more feasible and pragmatic to integrate its elements into the concerned subjects being taught at different school stages. Population education elements have accordingly been integrated in the selected subjects being taught at different school stages, such as Environmental Studies and Languages at the primary stage; Geography, Economics, Civics/Social Studies, Science and Languages at the upper primary and secondary stages; and Economics, Geography, Sociology, Political Science, History, Psychology, Biology/Life Sciences, Home Science and Languages at the higher secondary stage.

Moreover, attempts have also been made to include a separate paper on population education, over and above integrating its elements in existing papers in the pre-service elementary and secondary teacher education courses. As regards in-service teacher training, while independent training programmes for teachers of all the school stages have been extensively organised, elements of population education have also been dovetailed with the general in-service teacher training programmes being conducted by different institutions.

2.1.6. Co-curricular Approach

Co-curricular activities have always been an integral part of the teaching-learning process. Their significance particularly for an educational area like population education, which aims primarily at influencing attitude and behaviour of the learners, can hardly be over emphasised. However, for population education co-curricular activities are considered important not only for reinforcing the classroom teaching but also for initiating the teaching-learning process without waiting for a number of its elements to become an integral part of school syllabi and textbooks. The activities are expected to be organised in schools on such a scale and so frequently that both students and teachers, and in certain cases the parents also, are thoroughly exposed to the new population education contents.

2.1.7. Strategies for Curriculum Transaction

Adoption of appropriate strategies for curriculum transaction is crucial for achievement of the objectives of population education. It is very often presumed that when there is teaching, learning takes place automatically, and that learners learn only because the teacher teaches them. But this is not always true. There can be no learning, in spite of teaching, and the learners can learn even without teaching. As a matter of fact whether learning takes place, whether things learnt are retained and whether the learning process leads to desirable attitude formation and behaviour change depend largely on the teacher and the teaching methods.

This is more so for educational areas like population education, the primary focus of which is on the inculcation of positive attitude and the development of responsible behaviour towards population and development issues. The expository method of teaching, the lecture method or 'chalk and talk' method has serious limitations. There is a series of "new" methods known as "participatory" methods which have been considered very effective because of their potential to induce students into taking active participation in the teaching-learning process. In this context problem solving/discovery approach and value clarification strategies are found to be more functional.

References

Ehsanul Haq, *Sociology of Population in India*, Macmillan India, 2007

Grover R.P., and Ramesh Kumar Bhardwaj, *Population Education in India*, Ambala Cantt, The Associated Publishers, 2002.

Joseph Raju B., Gadde Annie Anitha and Digumarti Bhaskara Rao, *Population Education*, New Delhi, Sonali, 2004.

Kumarasena Harsha, *A Textbook of Population Education*, New Delhi, Dominant, 2004.

Lakshmi Narasaiah M., *Population and Education*, New Delhi, Discovery Publishing House, 2007.

Rajesh, *Population and Development Education in Indian Universities*, Delhi, Indian Publihers, 2004.

Tilottama Senapati, *Curriculum Development in Population Education*, New Delhi, Anmol Publishers, 2006.

Venkataiah S., *Population Education,* New Delhi, Anmol, 2001.

CHAPTER 3

Growth of World Population

3.1. Introduction

World population was transformed in the 20th century as technological and social changes brought steep declines in birth rates and death rates around the world. The century began with 1.6 billion people and ended with 6.1 billion, mainly because of unprecedented growth after 1960. The future of world population is less certain. Public discourse on population today tends to flow in one of two directions. One emphasises the continued growth in the less developed regions, and the economic, social, environmental, and political strains associated with adding a few billion more people in the next 50 years. The other focus centers around the unprecedented low fertility in many countries.

About 40 percent of the world's population lives in countries in which couples have so few children that the countries' populations are likely to decline over the long term. These countries, which include China and most of Europe, must grapple with social, economic, environmental, and political challenges associated with aging and eventually dwindling populations. And, if fertility rates continue to fall around the world, more countries will face this low-fertility predicament.

Nearly all future population growth will occur in the developing regions of the world. Urban areas in these regions will absorb most of the additional people. Population is growing fastest among the poorest population groups within developing countries. In these countries, a "youth bulge" ensures that the absolute number of births will rise even as couples are having fewer children.

At the other extreme, most countries in Europe now have a "youth dearth" after decades of low fertility. Stagnant growth or even population decline is challenging more countries as fewer workers must support expanding pension and social security systems for their aging citizens.

Governments have crafted a range of population policies to address these and other issues over the last half-century. In developing countries, policies include support for family planning and reproductive health programmes and efforts to improve women's status, to enable women to have the number of children they want. In developed countries, particularly Japan and parts of Europe, governments have implemented policies to promote gender equality in the workplace and ease the burden of childrearing-all to encourage women to have more children.

The factors that drive childbearing trends-such as the economy, education, gender relations, and access to family planning-are numerous and complex, and public policies and programmes to influence population trends must address many issues at once. Demographic changes often take years to be evident, making it difficult to predict how today's actions will affect the future size and distribution of populations. Small changes in childbearing trends today have huge implications for future population size.

3.2. Transitions in the 20th Century

The different demographic situations facing developed and developing countries today reflect the population trends of the 20th century, and especially the past 50 years. These trends not only shaped the current profile of these countries' populations, but also will influence their demographic futures.

The 20th century can be viewed as a triumph for human health. Death rates plummeted and life expectancy soared first in the more developed countries, and then in much of the less developed world. Although fertility also fell in many areas, the sudden decline in mortality fuelled unprecedented population growth as births far exceeded deaths each year.

This uneven regional growth reduced the developed countries' share of world population from one-third to one-fifth over the century. Europe's relative share of world population fell most. In 1900, about one- quarter of the world's population lived in Europe; by 2000, barely one-eighth lived in Europe. In contrast, the less developed countries in Africa, Latin America, and the Caribbean accounted for more than one-fifth of the world in 2000-up from one-eighth in 1900. Asia contained nearly three-fifths of the total population by century's end.

3.2.1. Trends in Developed Countries

As the 20th century began, the more developed countries were well into the shift from high to low mortality and fertility known as the demographic transition.

In 1900, life expectancy at birth was 47 years in the United States and between 45 and 50 years in Europe, Japan, and Australia. Life expectancy would reach remarkably high levels by mid-century. U.S. life expectancy at birth shot up to 68 years by 1950 and reached 77 years by 2000. Average life expectancy rose even higher in Japan and many European countries, and it continues to improve. Infants and young children benefited most from this health transition. The infant mortality rate was below 60 in developed countries by the 1950s, and below 10 by 2000.

3.2.2. Exceptions

Russia and several other Central Asian and Eastern European countries have been the exceptions to this general improvement in health and mortality in the last 50 years. Male life expectancy began to slip during the 1960s in Russia. After a temporary improvement in the early 1980s, life expectancy fell again during the late 1980s and early 1990s, when the Soviet Union was dissolving and economic conditions were deteriorating. Between 1990 and 2000, Russian male life expectancy at birth fell from 64 to 59 years. Female life expectancy at birth dropped about two years to an average of 72 years.

The 1990s also saw marked increases in HIV/IDS and other infectious diseases, which exacted a further toll on the region's health. Analysts disagree about why the health status has declined, but many point to inadequate health services, lack of prescription medicine, high rates of smoking, poor nutrition, and increased alcohol and drug abuse.

3.2.3. Declining Fertility

Birth rates fell in most developed countries during the late 19th century. American women were having four children, on average, at the dawn of the 20th century, down from about seven in the early 1800s. Fertility declined further after 1900. Well before modern contraceptives were available, the total fertility rate fell to about two children per woman in the United States and even lower in Europe during the world economic crises of the 1930s. The protracted fertility declines after 1970 coincided with trends toward delayed marriage, more divorce, and an increase in the percentage of women going to college and working outside the home. The TFRs in many European countries fell below 2 children per woman by 1980. By 2000, the TFR was below 2.1 in almost all developed countries, including the United States, and had sunk to 1.2 or less in the Czech Republic, Italy, Spain, and several other countries. Although these extremely low TFRs may be a temporary adjustment to changing socioeconomic conditions, the UN assumes TFRs will stay below 2.0 in developed countries in coming decades.

The sustained low fertility in Europe was not foreseen in the classic demographic transition theory, which assumed that fertility would stabilise at replacement level and population growth would cease over the long term. The current low fertility will lead to population decline for Europe unless there is massive immigration.

The United States-the most populous developed country-has had higher fertility than most other developed countries for the past 25 years. The ethnic and racial diversity of Americans and the substantial immigration from countries where large families are the norm explain part, but not all, of the higher U.S. fertility. After falling briefly below 1.8 in the mid-1970s, the U.S. TFR has hovered around for the past decade.

3.2.4. Trends in Less Developed Countries

In the early 20th century, most of Africa, Asia, and Latin America were still in the predemographic transition state of high mortality and high fertility. The course of Mexico's birth and death rates over the century illustrates the situation in many less developed countries-though the speed and timing of decline varied substantially. Mortality decline in some areas has been slowed or reversed by the spread of HIV/AIDS infection. AIDS mortality has reduced life expectancy in some countries of sub-Saharan Africa, and infection rates are increasing rapidly in South and East Asia. Although the epidemic has affected all world regions, it has exacted its greatest loss of life in the poorest countries-at least 98 percent of the roughly 3 million HIV/AIDS-related deaths in 2003 were in sub-Saharan Africa and other less developed regions.

In some regions, a high prevalence of sexually transmitted infections increases susceptibility to HIV/AIDS and contributes to widespread infertility. While surveys suggest that most women in developing countries have more children than they would like, infertility prevents other women from having as many as they want, causing economic and social problems for families.

Fertility has fallen in most developing countries, but the paths to lower fertility have varied. In 2003, the TFR in Asia stood at about 2.6, less than one-half its 1950 level; the TFR for Latin America and the Caribbean was down to 2.7 from 5.9 in 1950. Fertility also fell in Africa, but it remains well above the average for any other region.

China represents one extreme of the childbearing patterns in the developing world: countries that have completed a transition to belowreplacement fertility. The TFR is also near or below 2.1 in Brazil, Costa Rica, Korea, and Thailand. Including China, one-fourth of the population in the developing world lives in countries with below-replacement fertility. Momentum from a young age structure ensures continued growth for these countries, but the momentum will eventually subside and population size will stabilise or decline if these countries hold to their low fertility path.

At the other extreme are countries where fertility has remained high. Most of these countries are in the Middle East (Yemen) or in extremely poor regions of sub-Saharan Africa (Congo, Uganda), and they make up less than 5 percent of world population.

Asia includes many of the most populous countries in this middle group, including Bangladesh, India, Indonesia, Pakistan, and the Philippines. In India, as in many countries, periods of fertility decline have been interrupted by plateaus. Most of Latin America is also in this middle range. Brazil and Costa Rica are on the lower end, with TFRs near replacement level. On the high end, a handful of Latin American countries, including Bolivia, Guatemala, Haiti, and Paraguay, had moderately high TFRs between 4.1 and 4.7 in 2003.

Sub-Saharan Africa is a high-fertility region-though fertility has declined and is continuing to decline in many of the region's countries. Accordingly, Africa's future growth is subject to wide speculation. Many demographers detect a transition to lower fertility in much of the region but disagree about how fast and how far fertility will decline. Africa's widespread poverty, high rates of illiteracy, largely rural populations, and strong traditional preferences for large families do not favour a rapid decline. In addition, some public health professionals fear that the HIV/AIDS pandemic has siphoned off public health funds that might have gone to expand family planning services for women, and could delay the fertility transition. Fertility has remained stubbornly high in Mali, Niger, and Uganda, and may have risen in Kenya in the early 2000s.

The course of demographic transition also is not clear in the Middle East, which includes North Africa and parts of Western Asia. Fertility remains generally high despite impressive declines in mortality, but the situation varies throughout the region. Mortality fell rapidly in the oil-producing Persian Gulf states, because of improved public health, expanded education, and higher incomes brought by oil revenues. But the traditional culture in countries such as Yemen favours large families, and fertility has remained high.

3.3. Immigration and Urbanisation

Fertility and mortality drive most demographic change, but migration within and between countries also affects population growth. Migration affects the distribution of the population by age, sex, cultural, racial, and other characteristics in the communities that send and that receive migrants. Throughout the 20th century, the largest migration flows involved individuals and families moving from rural to urban areas. The major shift of population from rural to urban areas began during the late 19th century, when Europe and North America were industrialising, and when faster and better communication made it easier for people to move. Economic development and trade were centered in urban areas, and cities offered better job opportunities, amenities, and public services than villages and rural areas. By 1950, more than one-half (55 percent) of the residents of more developed countries lived in urban areas, up from about one-quarter in 1900. In 2000, about three-quarters (75 percent) lived in urban areas.

In most of Africa, Asia, and Latin America, life was centered in the countryside for much of the 20th century. Just 18 percent of developing country residents lived in urban areas in 1950. As these regions began to industrialise, rural residents began moving to the cities. These rural migrants fostered industrial development by enlarging the urban labour pool, as had their counterparts in Europe and the United States decades earlier. The flow began slowly but soon expanded into an unprecedented wave, helped by improved communication and transportation networks and increased population growth in rural areas.

Urban residents usually have higher educational levels, lower fertility, higher incomes, better health, and longer lives than rural residents. Thus, urbanisation appears to accelerate the demographic transition to lower mortality and fertility. Cities offer many amenities and economies of scale that lower the costs of providing public services. But the unprecedented population growth in urban areas in the past 50 years has strained the capacity of many less developed countries to provide basic services for all but the most privileged residents, and there is a growing gap between rich and poor in the urban areas of many countries.

3.3.1. Global Migration

About 175 million people-about 3 percent of world population-are international migrants: They live in a country other than their country of birth. This pool of international migrants is fluid; many migrants move back to their native country, while new migrants arrive. The migrant pool is augmented by an estimated 5 million to 10 million people each year. A large majority of international migrants are from less developed countries-not surprising since about 80 percent of world population lives in these countries. Most people move to take advantage of better economic opportunities, but some 14 million international migrants are refugees or asylees who were forced from their home countries by political violence or the threat of persecution. In the late 1990s and early 2000s millions left Afghanistan for Iran and Pakistan- although many later returned. Refugees often return to their home countries when conditions stabilise.

Migration flows from the less developed to the more developed countries include the movement from South and Central America to North America, and from North Africa and the Middle East to Europe. The flow from Asia to North America and Australia has also accelerated. Immigration makes up a significant part of the population growth in countries in which fertility has sunk so low that annual deaths outnumber annual births. Large and sustained migrant flows can alter the fertility levels in receiving countries when migrants come from countries with higher fertility norms.

Immigration can also introduce new health issues, such as infectious diseases or chronic health problems endemic in the countries of origin but less common in the countries of destination. Migration, in concert with fertility and mortality, changes population size and characteristics. Some countries escape population decline only because of a sustained influx of migrants. Other countries reduce stress from rapid population growth through emigration.

Fertility, mortality, and migration trends are reflected in the age and sex profiles of the world's countries. Fertility has the greatest influence on population structure in nearly all countries. The decades of high fertility rates in the less developed countries have meant ever-increasing numbers of young people, illustrated by the broad base of the age-sex pyramid for West Africa.

Improvements in infant and child mortality also contributed to the expanding youth population, as greater proportions of each generation live to adulthood. The broad base of the West African population structure is a powerful force for future population growth, as these ever-larger cohorts of young people move into childbearing ages. The number of women of childbearing age, roughly ages 15 to 49, will rise from about 52 million to 151 million between 2000 and 2050.

The age structure of Western Europe, in contrast, reveals the effects of excessive deaths and dearth of births during World War II, a postwar baby boom, and then decades of low fertility. Almost every cohort born after 1965 was smaller than the one that preceded it. Occasional flows of immigrants-especially from Eastern and Southern Europe, North Africa, and the Middle East-have added to the middle-age bulge because most migrants enter as young adults. There are nearly as many older people as children in Western Europe and in many other developed regions. The under-15 age group made up about 17 percent of the 2000 population in Western Europe, while those age 65 or older made up about 16 percent.

The population age structure reflects the forces of the three demographic variables involved in any demographic change, but in the modern world, fertility is the major source of growth and change and warrants special attention.

3.3.2. Factors Influencing Child Birth

Recent population growth has been mainly determined by fertility, which, in turn, is influenced by a range of biological, cultural, and economic factors. Women are capable of bearing more than 15 children, but national averages never reach this level because social and economic factors directly or indirectly limit the number of children women have. These factors include physical or biological impairments (some related to age); marriage traditions; sexual mores; family size preferences; living arrangements; job opportunities; child-care options; and many others.

In societies where women marry young and where all childbearing takes place within marriage, changes in the age at marriage can significantly affect fertility. In societies where women breastfeed their babies for up to two years, postpartum infecundity affects fertility levels by delaying the next pregnancy. Prolonged breastfeeding is less common and therefore a less-important fertility constraint than it was a few decades ago, but it is still important in some parts of the world, especially in sub-Saharan Africa.

In most countries, contraceptive use and abortion are the main proximate determinants of fertility and account for most fertility differences between countries. The reasons why women use contraceptives more are related to education, income, women's roles, and other factors, as well as to government policies. The impact of abortion in a country depends on the availability of reliable contraception, cultural attitudes about abortion, and access to abortion. In some Eastern European countries, women often turn to abortion because modern contraceptives can be difficult to obtain, of poor quality, and not promoted by policymakers or the medical community. In contrast, abortion is generally legal, relatively unrestricted, and available at little or no cost.

In societies with very low fertility and easy access to modern contraceptives, cultural and economic factors explain most of the fertility differences among countries. Women in these countries usually have fewer children than they say they expect. Life experiences-lack of a stable partner, frustrated material aspirations, insecure or inflexible employment, and inadequate housing might cause women to revise their ideas about how many children to have, or to delay a pregnancy until they are past reproductive age. This mismatch between expectations and behaviour arising from lifestyles and experiences is sometimes referred to as "competition."

The gap between expected and actual fertility was greater in Italy, where the second demographic transition transformed society after World War II. Women gained opportunities in education and employment and postponed marriage and childbearing. Divorce became legal only in the 1970s and, although divorce laws are more restrictive in Italy than in most other European countries, divorce is increasing. In the 1970s and 1980s, young Italian women had greater individual choice and access to contraception and abortion than did earlier generations.

Yet Italians have maintained strong family and cultural traditions that discourage cohabitation and childbearing outside marriage-contrary to trends in the United States and northern Europe. In the United States and many European countries, one-third or more of all births occurred outside marriage as early as 1990. In Italy, less than one-tenth of births were outside marriage by the late 1990s. Young Italian men and women remain single and live in their parents' homes longer than Americans or most other young Europeans. Italian women wait longer to have children than American women. The struggle between traditional values and contemporary social reality in Italy helped push fertility to unprecedented lows in the past decade.

3.3.3. Education

Around the world, more young people are enrolling in school and advancing their educations. This welcome trend is likely to affect health and fertility in developing countries because women with more education wait longer to have children and tend to have smaller, healthier families. Women with more education usually have their first sexual experience later, marry later, want smaller families, and are more likely to use contraception than their less-educated counterparts. Among Peruvian women ages 20 to 29 in the 1990s only 17 percent of those with seven or more years of education had a baby by age 20, while 60 percent who completed fewer than seven years of education had a baby by age 20.

In countries with poor living conditions and low literacy levels, gaining a little education is not always associated with lower fertility. In some poor countries, women with a few years of schooling had at least as many children as women with no education. In these settings, gaining any formal education is associated with higher incomes and better nutrition, which enhances women's ability to bear children. But women who completed at least seven years of education had far fewer children than less educated women, suggesting that seven years of education may be a threshold for significant fertility decline in poor countries with low literacy levels.

The context in which education takes place is critical in shaping childbearing decisions. Fertility tends to decline more rapidly where schooling is widespread or primary school enrolment is nearly universal. Schools and education-related activities often help spread attitudes about the benefits of smaller families throughout a community. As overall education levels rise, social norms concerning childbearing and parenting can change even for women without much formal education. The costs of having children also rise when primary education becomes universal-not only do parents sometimes have to pay school fees for each child, they also lose potential labour that children could provide. Other factors, such as exposure to mass media, access to family planning services, and job opportunities for women, are also associated with fertility declines, even without universal education.

Women's education is also associated with better child health. Educated women may have higher status within their families and communities than women with no education, and their higher status makes them more effective at negotiating for better care for their children. In developing countries, women with some formal education are more likely to obtain care during pregnancy, to immunise their children, and to take appropriate action when a child becomes ill. Further, in most societies, children of mothers with some education have a lower risk of dying than do children whose mothers had no education.

Education clearly affects the age at childbearing in low-fertility countries. It usually brings women more employment options; a few years of education can result in smaller family size when the education provides access to a job that offers a promising alternative to early marriage and childbearing. Universal education can also make it more difficult for women to combine working and large families because older children are in school and not available to care for younger siblings. Many women postpone having children until they have completed their educations and established their careers. This delay in childbearing is the cause of the tempo effect that has kept fertility low in most developed countries.

Traditional explanations for the relationship between education and fertility emphasise the trade-offs between women having children or taking advantage of employment opportunities opened up by a good education. But this relationship is not always straightforward because many other variables determine whether and how much women work for pay, including the local economy, availability of child care, and social attitudes about mothers in the workplace.

3.3.4. Income

Income is clearly linked to fertility levels across and within countries. Women in richer countries generally have fewer children than women in poorer ones. The exceptions to this relationship are the rich oil-producing states of the Middle East, where cultural traditions that foster low status for women also support high fertility.

Income levels and poverty thresholds are difficult to compare among countries, but a recent study on the relationship between income and health in developing countries uses household asset data from the Demographic and Health Surveys (DHS) programme-a survey research project operating in Africa, Asia, and Latin America-to measure wealth. The study develops an asset index based on measures such as ownership of a refrigerator, television or radio, car, motorcycle, or bicycle; the household's construction material, size, and source for drinking water; and the type of toilet facilities. The resulting household asset index reflects a country-specific or relative definition of economic status rather than an absolute measure.

3.3.5. Gender Roles

In high- and low-fertility countries, fertility is influenced by the relative power held by men and women and the dynamics of the relations between them. Gender norms affect fertility in many ways. In societies in which women have lower literacy and less access than men to mass media, women may know relatively little about reproductive health, including how to avoid unwanted pregnancies. Where men have more power than women, women may find it hard to negotiate contraceptive use. In lowfertility countries, fertility is lowest where women combine full-time employment with most of the household and childrearing responsibilities. Fertility is higher where women have more support from their spouses for housework and childrearing, access to government-provided family support resources, or both.

Son preference is another manifestation of gender norms that can influence fertility levels. In several South Asian and Middle Eastern countries, couples may continue to have children until they have a son, thereby pushing up overall fertility.

3.4. Population and Development

The relationship among demographic variables, income, and gender is highly complex-and it is tied to the broader question of how population size and the pace of population growth affect economic development. For decades, experts have debated the impact of rapid population growth on economic development.

Population pessimists have insisted that high fertility and rapid population growth inhibit development. This view contributed to the rationale for widespread funding of family planning policies and programmes in the 1960s. Conversely, population optimists have argued that rapid population growth and large population size can promote economic prosperity by furnishing abundant human and intellectual capital and by increasing market size. In the 1980s, a third view, population neutralism, gained prominence, supported by a sizable body of economic research showing little evidence that population growth by itself affects economic performance. But measuring the impact of population on the economy is complicated by many factors, such as economic cycles and financial crises.

The focus on population size and growth has largely ignored a critical demographic variable: the age structure of the population. Because individual economic behaviour varies at different stages of life, changes in age structure can significantly affect national economic performance. Nations with a high proportion of young or old dependents tend to devote a relatively high proportion of resources to these groups, often limiting economic growth. By contrast, nations in which a relatively large share of the population has reached the prime ages for working and saving may enjoy a boost to income growth stemming from the higher share of the population that is working, from the accelerated accumulation of capital, and from reduced spending on dependents. This phenomenon, known as the demographic dividend, can arise in countries that have a sharp decline in fertility. The combined effect of this dividend and effective policies in other areas can stimulate economic growth.

Declining mortality, followed by declines in fertility, resulted in a rapid demographic transition in East Asia between 1965 and 1990. As a result, the working-age population grew four times faster than the dependent (youth and elderly) population. Strong educational systems and greater international trade have enabled national economies to absorb this "boom" generation into the work force. The demographic dividend fuelled the region's spectacular economic boom: Real per capita income growth averaged 6 percent per year between 1965 and 1990. The demographic dividend accounted for approximately one-fourth to two-fifths of this growth.

As the East Asian case shows, falling fertility rates can create conditions for economic growth. Effective family planning can accelerate the demographic transition, potentially enhancing economic benefits and lifting nations out of a cycle of poverty. However, reduced fertility by itself provides no guarantee of prosperity.

3.4.1. Responses to Population Growth

Concerns about rapid population growth and overpopulation have a long history. English economist Thomas Malthus wrote a famous treatise on the subject in 1798, arguing that growing populations would outstrip food supplies, resulting in poverty, famine, and death. Almost 200 years later in the United States, the publication of Paul Ehrlich's The Population Bomb in 1968 stimulated widespread media coverage and public debate about the harmful consequences of rapid population growth. The dire predictions of these and other writers have generated both support and criticism over the years, as well as lingering questions about the consequences of future growth.

3.4.2. Growing Influence of Women's Groups

In the late 1980s and early 1990s, women's health and rights advocates became increasingly concerned about many governments' apparent interest -even obsession-in promoting family planning to stabilise population growth. They asserted that government-funded programmes were distributing contrace-ptives with little regard for the health of women who used them. Especially in Asia, where governments were the largest providers of services, family planning programmes were administered and evaluated based on targets and quotas for "family planning acceptors." Women's rights advocates opposed top-down, target-driven approaches to slowing population growth. They maintained that these approaches promote coercion and violate women's right to reproductive freedom. Programmes based on targets and quotas, the groups argued, tend to emphasise numerical goals at the expense of service quality and women's reproductive choices.

References

Cromartie, Michael (e.d.), *The Nine Lives of Population Control*, Grand Rapids (MI): Ethics and Public Policy Center and Wm. B. Eerdmans Publishing Co. 1995.

Eberstadt, Nicholas, "The Population Implosion," in *The Wall Street Journal*, Thursday October 16, 1997.

Hartmann, Betsy, *Reproductive Rights & Wrongs: The Global Policies of Population Control*, Boston: South End Press 1995.

Pritchett, Lant H., "Desired Fertility and the Impact of Population Policies," in *Population and Development Review*, Vol.20 (no.1), March 1994.

Kasun, Jacqueline, *The War Against Population*, San Francisco: Ignatius Press 1988.

Simon, Julian L., *Population Matters*, New Brunswick (NJ): Transaction Publishers, 1990.

Wattenberg, Ben, "The Population Explosion is Over," in *The New York Times Magazine*, Nov. 23, 1997.

CHAPTER 4

Theories of Population

4.1. Malthusian Theory of Population

Thomas Robert Malthus was an English demographer and political economist. He is best known for his highly influential views on population growth. Thomas Robert Malthus was born to Daniel and Henrietta Malthus, the sixth of seven children.

4.1.1. Malthusian Principles

Malthus's views were largely developed in reaction to the optimistic views of his father and his associates, notably Rousseau. Malthus's essay was also in response to the views of the Marquis de Condorcet. In 1798 Malthus famously predicted that population would outrun food supply, leading to a decrease in food per person. He even went so far as to specifically predict that this must occur by the middle of the 19th century, a prediction which failed for several reasons, including his use of static analysis, taking recent trends and projecting them indefinitely into the future, which often fails for complex systems. The advent of industrial chemistry and use of chemical fertilisers did much to increase crop yields and food availability.

According to Malthus, "The power of population is so superior to the power of the earth to produce subsistence for man, that premature death must in some shape or other visit the human race. The vices of mankind are active and able ministers of depopulation. They are the precursors in the great army of destruction, and often finish the dreadful work themselves. But should they fail in this war of extermination, sickly seasons, epidemics, pestilence, and plague advance in terrific array, and sweep off their thousands and tens of thousands. Should success be still incomplete, gigantic inevitable famine stalks in the rear, and with one mighty blow levels the population with the food of the world."

This Principle of Population was based on the idea that population if unchecked increases at a geometric rate (i.e. 2, 4, 8, 16, etc.) whereas the food supply grows at an arithmetic rate (i.e. 1, 2, 3, 4, etc.).

Only natural causes (e.g. accidents and old age), misery (war, pestilence, and above all famine), moral restraint and vice (which for Malthus included infanticide, murder, contraception and homosexuality) could check excessive population growth.

Malthus favoured moral restraint (including late marriage and sexual abstinence) as a check on population growth. However, it is worth noting that Malthus proposed this only for the working and poor classes. Thus, the lower social classes took a great deal of responsibility for societal ills, according to his theory. In his work *An Essay on the Principle of Population*, he proposed the gradual abolition of poor laws. Essentially what this resulted in was the promotion of legislation which degenerated the conditions of the poor in England, lowering their population but effectively decreasing poverty.

Malthus himself noted that many people misrepresented his theory and took pains to point out that he did not just predict future catastrophe. Malthus regarded his Principle of Population as an explanation of the past and the present situation of humanity as well as a prediction of our future.

Additionally, many have argued that Malthus did not fully recognise the human capacity to increase food supply. So, Malthus was of the opinion that the main peculiarity which distinguishes man from other animals, is the means of his support, is the power which he possesses of very greatly increasing these means.

However, it should be noted that the explosion in human population is strongly correlated with the discovery and extraction of hydrocarbons. Hydrocarbon technology is the primary means by which food supply has increased since the 19th century through fertiliser derived from natural gas feedstock and mechanisation and transport enabled by liquid fuels. The peaking of world hydrocarbon production (Peak oil) may test Malthus's critics. While critics may be justified that a global famine has not occurred, such events should be contrasted with famines throughout history.

4.1.2. Population Predictions of Malthus

Malthus predicted continuing famines in Europe which has been proved false. Some claim that there is no specific prediction of Malthus regarding the future; that what some interpret as prediction was merely Malthus's illustration of the power of geometric (or exponential) population growth compared to the arithmetic growth of food production. Rather than a prediction of the future, the Essay is an evolutionary social theory.

It is this theory of Malthus that has had huge influence on evolutionary theory in both biology and the social sciences. Malthus's population theory has also profoundly affected the modern day ecological-evolutionary social theory of Gerhard Lenski and Marvin Harris. He can thus be regarded as a key contributing element of the canon of socioeconomic theory.

Malthus argued that as wages increase within a country, the birthrate increases while the death rate decreases. His reasoning was that high incomes allowed people to have sufficient means to raise their children such as feeding and clothing them thus resulting in greater desire to have more children which increases the population. In addition, high incomes also allowed people to be able to afford proper medication to fight off potentially harmful diseases thus decreasing the death rate. As a result, wage increases caused population to grow as the birthrate increases and the death rate decreases. He further argued that as the supply of labor increases with the increased population growth at a constant labor demand, the wages earned would decrease eventually to subsistence where the birthrate is equal to the death rate resulting in no population growth. However, the world generally has experienced quite a different result than the one Malthus predicted with his theory.

During the late 19th and early 20th century, the population increased as did the wages, with the spread of the industrial revolution. Malthus assumed a constant labor demand in his assessment of England and in doing so he ignored the effects of industrialisation. As the world became more industrialised, the level of technology and production grew causing an increase in labor demand. Thus, even though labour supply increased so did the demand for labour. In fact, the labour demand arguably increased more than the supply, as measured by the historically observed increase in real wages globally with population growth.

4.1.3. Neo-Malthusianism

Neo-malthusianism is a set of doctrines derived from Thomas Malthus's theory that limited resources keep populations in check and reduce economic growth. Current proponent of Neo-

Malthusianism is the Club of Rome. Scholars working with the original Malthus Theory included the advocated use of contraception to the theory which formed the basic views of Neo-Malthusianism.

Malthus believed population growth was exponential, and agricultural growth was arithmetic; therefore, population growth will increase at such a rate that eventually there won't be enough food for the subsistence of the population. This appears to describe rather accurately sociodemographic dynamics of complex pre-industrial societies and serves as a basis for modern mathematical models of long-term historical dynamics.

4.1.4. Influence

The influence of Malthus's theory of population was substantial. High fertility had been considered an economic advantage, since it increased the number of workers available to the economy. Malthus, however, looked at fertility from a new perspective and convinced most economists that even though high fertility might increase the gross output, it tended to reduce output per capita. Malthus has been widely admired by, and has influenced, a number of other notable economists such as David Ricardo and Alfred Marshall.

A distinguished early convert was British Prime Minister, William Pitt The Younger. In the 1830s Malthus's writings strongly influenced Whig reforms which overturned Tory paternalism and brought in the Poor Law Amendment Act of 1834. Concerns about Malthus's theory also helped promote the idea of a national population Census in the UK. Government official John Rickman was instrumental in the first modern British Census being conducted in 1801.

Malthus's idea of man's "Struggle for existence" had decisive influence on Charles Darwin and the theory of evolution. Other scientists related this idea to plants and animals which helped to define a piece of the evolutionary puzzle. This struggle for existence of all creatures is the catalyst by which natural selection produces the "survival of the fittest", a phrase coined by Herbert Spencer. Darwin, in his book The Origin of Species, called his theory an application of the doctrines of Malthus in an area without the complicating factor of human intelligence. Darwin referred to Malthus as "that great philosopher" and wrote in his notebook that "Malthus on Man should be studied".

Darwin recognised the significance of competition between populations of the same species, as well as competition between species. Malthusian population thinking also explained how an incipient species could become a full-blown species in a very short time frame.

Founder of UNESCO, evolutionist and Humanist, Julian Huxley was openly critical of Communist and Roman Catholic attitudes to birth control, population control and overpopulation. Today world organisations such as the United Nations Population Fund acknowledge that the debate over how many people the Earth can support effectively started with Malthus. Julian's brother, author Aldous Huxley, in his book Brave New World, refers to Malthusian theories on population. In Brave New World, the popular form of birth control is known as the Malthusian Belt. It is mentioned frequently by the females in the novel including the female protagonist Lenina Crowne.

Karl Marx's social determinism has its roots in Malthus's theory as well. Marx however rejected Darwin's biological determinism and instead embraced social determinism. He saw social ills as caused by unjust or faulty institutions and social arrangements in large part caused by capitalism. Malthus continues to have considerable influence to this day. More recently, a school of "neo-Malthusian" scholars has begun to link population and economics to a third variable, political change and political violence, and to show how the variables interact. In the early 1980s, James Goldstone linked population variables to the English Revolution and David Lempert devised a model of demographics, economics, and political change in the multi-ethnic country of Mauritius. Goldstone has since modeled other revolutions by looking at demographics and economics and Lempert has explained Stalin's purges and the Russian Revolution of 1917 in terms of demographic factors that drive political economy.

Malthus is widely regarded as the founder of modern demography. Malthus had proposed his Principle of Population as a universal natural law for all species, not just humans. Instead, today, his theory is widely regarded as only an approximate natural law of population dynamics for all species. This is because it can be proven that nothing can sustain exponential growth at a constant rate indefinitely.

Nonetheless, Malthus continues to openly inspire and influence even futuristic visions, such as those of K Eric Drexler relating to space advocacy and molecular nanotechnology. The Malthusian growth model now bears Malthus's name. His arithmetic model of food supply is disputed by some, as it is arguable that food supply has kept pace with population for the past two centuries.

"Malthusian" policy did not take account of the enormous economic damage done by famines through loss of human capital, collapse of credit structures and financial institutions, and the destruction of physical capital (especially in the form of livestock), social infrastructure and commercial relationships. The presumably unintended consequence was that production often did not recover to pre-famine levels in the affected areas for a decade or more after each disaster, well after the lost population had been regained. Malthusian theory also influenced British policies in Ireland during the 1840s, in which relief measures during the Irish Potato Famine were neglected and mass starvation was seen as a natural and inevitable consequence of the island's supposed over-population.

Although it is popularly assumed that Malthus's pessimistic views gave economics the nickname "the Dismal Science", the phrase was actually coined by the historian Thomas Carlyle in reference to laissez-faire economic theories in general.

4.1.5. Criticism

Theoretical and political critiques of Malthus and Malthusian thinking emerged soon after the publication of the first Essay on Population, most notably in the work of the reformist industrialist Robert Owen, the essayist William Hazlitt and economists John Stuart Mill and Nassau William Senior, and moralist William Cobbett. Also of note was True Law of Population by politician Thomas Doubleday, an adherent of Cobbett's views.

4.1.5.1. Marxist

The highpoint of opposition to Malthus's ideas came in the middle of the nineteenth century with the writings of Karl Marx (Capital, 1867) and Friedrich Engels (Outlines of a Critique of Political Economy, 1844), who argued that what Malthus saw as the problem of the pressure of population on the means of production was actually that of the pressure of the means of production on population. They thus viewed it in terms of their concept of the labor reserve army. In other words, the seeming excess of population that Malthus attributed to the seemingly innate disposition of the poor to reproduce beyond their means was actually a product of the very dynamic of capitalist economy.

4.1.5.2. Evolutionist

Evolutionists Smith and Ronald Fisher were both critical of Malthus's hypothesis, though it was Fisher who referred to the growth rate as the Malthusian parameter. Smith doubted that famine was the great leveler that Malthus insisted it was.

4.1.5.3. Cornucopian

Some 19th century economists believed that improvements in the division and specialisation of labour, increased capital investment, and other factors had rendered some of Malthus's warnings implausible. In the absence of any improvement in technology or increase of capital equipment, an increased supply of labour may have a synergistic effect on productivity that overcomes the law of diminishing returns. Many 20th century economists, such as Julian Lincoln Simon, noted that despite the predictions of Malthus and the Neo-Malthusians, massive geometric population growth in the 20th century has not resulted in a Malthusian catastrophe, largely due to the influence of technological advances and the expansion of the market economy, division of labor, and stock of capital goods.

The oncoming peaking of global oil production (and subsequent decline of production), along with the peak of North American natural gas production will very likely precipitate this agricultural crisis much sooner than expected. Geologist Dale Allen Pfeiffer claims that coming decades could see spiraling food prices without relief and massive starvation on a global level such as never experienced before.

4.2. Herbert Spencer

Herbert Spencer (27 April 1820 - 8 December 1903) was an English philosopher and prominent classic-liberal political theorist. He developed an all-embracing conception of evolution as the progressive development of the physical world, biological organisms, the human mind, and human culture and societies. The lifelong bachelor contributed to a wide range of subjects, including ethics, metaphysics, religion, politics, rhetoric, biology, sociology, and psychology.

He is best known for coining the term survival of the fittest, which he did in Social Statics, before Charles Darwin's The Origin of Species. This term strongly suggests natural selection, yet as Spencer extended evolution into realms of sociology and ethics he made use of Lamarckism rather than natural selection.

4.2.1. Synthetic Philosophy

Spencer's philosophical system seemed to demonstrate that it was possible to believe in the ultimate perfection of humanity on the basis of advanced scientific conceptions such as the first law of thermodynamics and biological evolution.

In essence Spencer's philosophical vision was formed by a combination of Deism and Positivism. On the one hand, he had imbibed something of eighteenth century Deism from his father and other members of the Derby Philosophical Society and from books like George Combe's immensely popular The Constitution of Man. This treated the world as a cosmos of benevolent design, and the laws of nature as the decrees of a 'Being transcendentally kind.' Natural laws were thus the statutes of a well governed universe that had been decreed by the Creator with the intention of promoting human happiness. Although Spencer lost his Christian faith as a teenager and later rejected any 'anthropomorphic' conception of the Deity, he nonetheless held fast to this conception at an almost sub-conscious level, particularly given that his education did not equip him to identify and challenge his own assumptions. At the same time, however, he owed far more than he would ever acknowledge to Positivism, in particular in its conception of a philosophical system as the unification of the various branches of scientific knowledge. He also followed Positivism in his insistence that it was only possible to have genuine knowledge of phenomena and hence that it was idle to speculate about the nature of the ultimate reality. The tension between Positivism and his residual Deism ran through the entire System of Synthetic Philosophy.

Spencer followed Comte in aiming for the unification of scientific truth; it was in this sense that his philosophy aimed to be 'synthetic.' Like Comte, he was committed to the universality of natural law, the idea that the laws of nature applied without exception, to the organic realm as much as to the inorganic, and to the human mind as much as to the rest of creation. The first objective of the Synthetic Philosophy was thus to demonstrate that there were no exceptions to being able to discover scientific explanations, in the form of natural laws, of all the phenomena of the universe. Spencer's volumes on biology, psychology, and sociology were all intended to demonstrate the existence of natural laws in these specific disciplines. Even in his writings on ethics, he held that it was possible to discover 'laws' of morality that had the status of laws of nature while still having normative content, a conception which can be traced to Combe's Constitution of Man.

The second objective of the Synthetic Philosophy was to show that these same laws led inexorably to Progress. In contrast to Comte, who stressed only the unity of scientific method, Spencer sought the unification of scientific knowledge in the form of the reduction of all natural laws to one fundamental law, the law of evolution. In this respect, he followed the model laid down by the Edinburgh publisher Robert Chambers in his anonymous Vestiges of the Natural History of Creation. Although often dismissed as a lightweight forerunner of Charles Darwin's The Origin of Species, Chambers' book was in reality a programme for the unification of science which aimed to exhibit Laplace's Nebular Hypothesis for the origin of the solar system and Lamarck's theory of species transformation as both instantiations of 'one magnificent generalisation of progressive development.' Chambers was associated with Chapman's salon and his work served as the unacknowledged template for the Synthetic Philosophy.

4.2.2. Sociology

The evolutionary progression from simple, undifferentiated homogeneity to complex, differentiated, heterogeneity was exemplified, Spencer argued, by the development of society. He developed a theory of two types of society, the militant and the industrial, which corresponded to this evolutionary progression. Militant society, structured around relationships of hierarchy and obedience, was simple and undifferentiated; industrial society, based on voluntary, contractually assumed social obligations, was complex and differentiated. Society, which Spencer conceptualised as a 'social organism' evolved from the simpler state to the more complex according to the universal law of evolution. Moreover, industrial society was the direct descendant of the ideal society developed in Social Statics, although Spencer now equivocated over whether the evolution of society would result in anarchism or whether it pointed to a continued role for the state, albeit one reduced to the minimal functions of the enforcement of contracts and external defence.

4.2.3. Ethics

The end point of the evolutionary process would be the creation of 'the perfect man in the perfect society' with human beings becoming completely adapted to social life, as predicted in Spencer's first book. Because human instincts had a specific location in strands of brain tissue, they were subject to the Lamarckian mechanism of use-inheritance so that gradual modifications could be transmitted to future generations. Over the course of many generations the evolutionary process would ensure that human beings would become less aggressive and increasingly altruistic, leading eventually to a perfect society in which no one would cause another person pain.

However, for evolution to produce the perfect individual it was necessary for present and future generations to experience the 'natural' consequences of their conduct. Only in this way would individuals have the incentives required to work on self-improvement and thus to hand an improved moral constitution to their descendants. Hence anything that interfered with the 'natural' relationship of conduct and consequence was to be resisted and this included the use of the coercive power of the state to relieve poverty, to provide public education, or to require compulsory vaccination. Although charitable giving was to be encouraged even it had to be limited by the consideration that suffering was frequently the result of individuals receiving the consequences of their actions. Hence too much individual benevolence directed to the 'undeserving poor' would break the link between conduct and consequence that Spencer considered fundamental to ensuring that humanity continued to evolve to a higher level of development.

Spencer adopted a utilitarian standard of ultimate value - the greatest happiness of the greatest number - and the culmination of the evolutionary process would be the maximisation of utility. In the perfect society individuals would not only derive pleasure from the exercise of altruism but would aim to avoid inflicting pain on others. They would also instinctively respect the rights of others, leading to the universal observance of the principle of justice - each person had the right to a maximum amount of liberty that was compatible with a like liberty in others. 'Liberty' was interpreted to mean the absence of coercion, and was closely connected to the right to private property.

4.2.4. Agnosticism

Spencer's reputation among the Victorians owed a great deal to his agnosticism, the claim that it is impossible for us to have certain knowledge of God and he rejected theology as representing the 'impiety of the pious.' He was to gain much notoriety from his repudiation of traditional religion, and was frequently condemned by religious thinkers for allegedly advocating atheism and materialism. Nonetheless, unlike Huxley, whose agnosticism was a militant creed directed at 'the unpardonable sin of faith', Spencer insisted that he was not concerned to undermine religion in the name of science, but to bring about a reconciliation of the two.

4.2.5. Social Darwinism

Spencer is now chiefly remembered for his political theory. Although he has been claimed as a precursor by Libertarians and philosophical anarchists practically all that now remains among the ashes of Spencer's reputation is that he was a Social Darwinist who applied the law of the survival of the fittest to society. Humanitarian impulses had to be resisted as nothing should be allowed to interfere with the severity of the social struggle for existence, the entire point of which was to produce winners and losers. This interpretation has its primary source in Richard Hofstadter's Social Darwinism in American Thought which is frequently cited in the secondary literature as an authoritative account of the Synthetic Philosophy. Through constant repetition Hofstadter's Spencer has taken on a life of his own, his views and arguments represented by the same few passages, usually cited not directly from the source but from Hofstadter's rather selective quotations.

However, to regard Spencer as any kind of Darwinian, even of the 'Social' variety, is a gross distortion. He could never bring himself to abandon the idea that evolution equated to progress, that it involved the unfolding of a pre-existent pattern, and that there would be a final resting point - 'equilibrium' - in which an ultimate state of perfection was attained. Darwinian natural selection, with its open-ended process of change based on random variations that prospered or failed depending on their adaptation to environmental conditions, was thus far removed from Spencer's vision of progressive development, and he struggled hard to find a place for it within his overall system. Against this background, his use of the theory of natural selection could never be more than window dressing as it threatened the reassuring myth of universal evolutionary progress and thus the scientific foundation for morality that he hoped to establish. In contrast to the harsh and unforgiving imperative that the weak must be made to go to the wall, his main political message was essentially an anti-political one about the efficacy of self-improvement rather than collective action in bringing about the promised future state of human perfection.

4.2.6. Political influence

Despite his reputation as a Social Darwinist, Spencer's political thought has been open to mulitple interpretations. His political philosophy could both provide inspiration to those who believed that individuals were masters of their fate, who should brook no interference from a meddling state, and those who believed that social development required a strong central authority.

4.3. Marxian Economics

Marxian economics refers to a body of economic thought stemming from the work of Karl Marx. The adherents of Marxian economics, particularly in academia, distinguish it from Marxism as a political ideology, arguing that Marx's approach to understanding the economy is intellectually valuable per se, independent of Marx's advocacy for revolutionary socialism or the inevitability of proletarian revolution. It does not lean entirely upon the work of Marx and other widely known Marxists, but may draw from a range of Marxist and non-Marxist sources. His work is seen as the basis for a viable analytic framework and an alternative to more conventional neoclassical economics.

4.3.1. Marx and Classical Economics

Marx's economics took as its starting point the work of the best-known economists of his day, the British classical economists. Among these economists were Adam Smith, Thomas Malthus, and David Ricardo.

Smith, in The Wealth of Nations, argued that the most important characteristic of a market economy was that it permitted a rapid growth in productive abilities. Smith claimed that a growing market stimulated a greater "division of labour" (i.e., specialisation of businesses and/or workers) and this, in turn, led to greater productivity. Although Smith generally said little about laborers, he did note that an increased division of labor could at some point cause harm to those whose jobs became narrower and narrower as the division of labor expanded.

Marx followed Smith by claiming that the most important beneficial economic consequence of capitalism was a rapid growth in productivity abilities. Marx also expanded greatly on the notion that labourers could come to harm as capitalism became more productive.

Ricardo developed a theory of distribution within capitalism, that is, a theory of how the output of society is distributed to classes within society. The most mature version of his theory, presented in On the Principles of Political Economy and Taxation, was based on a labor theory of value in which the value of any produced object is equal to the labor embodied in the objected. Also notable in Ricardo's economic theory was that profit was a deduction from society's output and that wages and profit were inversely related: an increase in profit came at the expense of a reduction in wages. Marx built much of the formal economic analysis found in Capital on Ricardo's theory of the economy.

4.3.2. Marx's Economic Theories

Marx's major work on political economy was Capital: A Critique of Political Economy (better known by the German title Das Kapital). Marx wrote other treatises on economics: Critique of Political Economy, one of his early works, was mostly incorporated into Capital. Under the labor theory of value, the direct value of a commodity stems solely from the socially necessary labor time invested in it. But commodities also have a use value and an exchange value. The use value of a carrot lies in eating it and no longer being hungry, while its exchange value might be found in the quantity of gold which it could be sold for.

However, capitalists do not pay workers the full value of the commodities they produce. The gap between the value a worker produces and his or her wages are a form of unpaid labor, known as surplus value. To Marx, this is wage slavery, a central feature of capitalism as a mode of production.

Moreover, Marx notes that markets tend to obscure the social relationships and processes of production, a phenomenon he termed commodity fetishism. Consumers see a commodity only in market terms. In looking to obtain something as private property, they consider only its exchange value, rather than its labor value.

4.3.3. Criticisms

Marx's value theory and law of the tendency of the rate of profit to fall are internally inconsistent. In other words, the critics allege that Marx drew conclusions that actually do not follow from his theoretical premises. Once these alleged errors are "corrected," his conclusion that aggregate price and profit are determined by, and equal to, aggregate value and surplus value no longer holds true. This result calls into question his theory that the exploitation of workers is the sole source of profit. Likewise, Marx's law of the tendency of the rate of profit to fall says that laborsaving technological changes tend to lower the economy-wide rate of profit. However, the "corrected" version of this law - Okishio's theorem - implies that such technological changes tend to raise the rate of profit.

The inconsistency allegations have been a prominent feature of Marxian economics and the debate surrounding it since the 1970s. Andrew Kliman argues that, since internally inconsistent theories cannot possibly be right, the inconsistency charges serve to legitimate the suppression of Marx's critique of political economy and current-day research based upon it, as well as the "correction" of Marx's alleged inconsistencies.

Critics who have alleged that Marx has been proved internally inconsistent include former and current Marxian and/or Sraffian economists, such as Paul Sweezy, Nobuo Okishio, Ian Steedman, John Roemer, Gary Mongiovi, and David Laibman, who wish the field to be grounded in their "correct" versions of Marxian economics instead of in Marx's critique of political economy in the original form in which he presented and developed it in Capital.

4.3.3.1. Austrian critics

The Austrian School was the first group of liberal economists to systematically challenge Marxian economics. This was partly a reaction to the Methodenstreit, an attack on the Hegelian doctrines of the Historical School. Some Marxist authors have attempted to portray the Austrian school as a "bourgeois reaction" to Marx. However, opponents argue that it could not have been a reaction, since Carl Menger wrote his Principles of Economics at almost the same time as Marx was completing Das Kapital.

The classical economists had shown little interest in such topics, and many of them did not even gain familiarity with Marx's ideas until well into the twentieth century.

4.3.3.2. Current theorising in Marxian economics

Marxian economics has been built upon by many others, beginning almost at the moment of Marx's death. The second and third volumes of Das Kapital were edited by his close associate Friedrich Engels, based on Marx's notes. Marx's Theories of Surplus value was edited by Karl Kautsky. Some economists draw on, or have drawn on, Marxian economics together with other theoretical perspectives, in an eclectic manner, or in order to synthesise them. Those who refer to non-mainstream, or heterodox, economics as a single entity often include Marxian economics within it.

References

Elwell, Frank W., "A Commentary on Malthus's 1798", *Essay on Population as Social Theory*, The Edwin Mellon Press, 2001.

Eric B. Ross, *The Malthus factor: population, poverty, and politics in capitalist development*, Zed Books, London. ISBN 1-85649-564-7, 1998.

Hollander, Samuel, *The Economics of Thomas Robert Malthus*, University of Toronto Press, 1997.

James, Patricia, *Population Malthus : his Life and Times*, Londen : Routledge and Kegan Paul, 1979.

Spencer, Herbert, *First Principles*, New York: D. Appleton and Company, 1897.

Shlomo Avineri, *The Social and Political Thought of Karl Marx*, Cambridge University Press, 1968.

CHAPTER 5

Factors of Population Growth

5.1. Introduction

The twentieth century witnessed an unprecedented rapid improvement in health care technologies and access to health care all over the world; as a result there was a steep fall in the mortality and steep increase in longevity. The population realised these changes and took steps to reduce their fertility but the decline in fertility was not so steep. As a result the global population has undergone a fourfold increase in a hundred years and has reached 6 billion. Demographers refer to these changes from stable population with high fertility and mortality to a new stability in population due to low fertility and mortality patterns as demographic transition.

5.2. Demographic Transition

Demographic transition occurs in four phases; of these the first three phases are characterised by population growth. In the first phase there is a fall in death rate and improvement in longevity; this leads to population growth. In the second phase there is a fall in birth rate but fall is less steep than fall in death rates and consequently there is population growth. In the third phase death rates plateau and replacement level of fertility is attained but the population growth continues because of the large size of population in reproductive age group. The fourth phase is characterised by fall in birth rate to below replacement level and reduction in the proportion of the population in reproductive age group; as a result of these changes population growth ceases and population stabilises. Experience in some of the developed countries suggest that in some societies even after attainment of stable population there may be a further decline in fertility so that there is a further reduction in the population- so called negative population growth phase of the demographic transition. Different countries in the world have entered the demographic transition at different periods of time; there are also substantial differences in the rate of demographic transition and time taken to achieve population stabilisation.

5.2.1. Global Population Scenario

In 1901 the world population was 1.6 billion. By 1960, it became 3 billion, and by 1987, 5 billion and in 1999, 6 billion. Currently, one billion people are added every 12 - 13 years. During the last decade there has been substantial decline in birth rate. The reasons for decline vary from society to society; urbanisation, rising educational attainment, increasing employment among women, lower infant mortality are some major factors responsible for growing desire for smaller families; increasing awareness and improved access to contraception have made it possible for the majority of the couple to achieve the desired family size. In some countries slowing of the population growth has been due to an increase in mortality (e.g. HIV related mortality in sub-saharan Africa). As a result of all these the decline in the global population growth during the nineties is steeper than the earlier predictions. Currently, the annual increment is about 80 million. It is expected to decrease to about 64 million by 2020 -25 and to 33 million by 2045 -50; 95 % of the growth of population occurs in developing countries. Most demographers believe that the current accelerated decline in population growth will continue for the next few decades and the medium projections of Population Division of United Nations, that the global population will grow to 8.9 billion by 2050 is likely to be achieved.

5.2.2. Changing age Structure of Population

During demographic transition along with the growth in number there are changes in the population age structure. While the importance of the population growth as a determinant of quality of life is universally understood, the profoundly serious consequences of changing age structure especially if it occurs too rapidly is not understood by many. Population pyramids graphically represent complex changes in age structure of the population so that it can be readily understood and interpreted. Currently nearly half of the global population is below 25 years of age and one sixth are in the age group 15-24. Their choices, efforts and lifestyles will determine not only the population growth but also future improvement in the quality of life in harmony with global ecology. In developed countries the reproductive age group population is relatively small; their fertility is low and the longevity at birth is high. Population profiles of these countries resemble a cylinder and not a pyramid. These countries have the advantages of having achieved a stable population but have to face the problems of having a relatively small productive workforce to support the large aged population with substantial non-communicable disease burden. Some of the developing countries have undergone a very rapid decline in the birth rates within a short period. This enabled them to quickly achieve population stabilisation but they do face the problems of rapid changes in the age structure and workforce, which may be inadequate to meet their manpower requirements. In contrast the population in most of the developing countries (including India) consist of a very large proportion of children and persons in reproductive age. Because of the large reproductive age group (Population momentum) the population will continue to grow even when replacement level of fertility is reached (couples having only two children). It is imperative that these countries should generate enough employment opportunities for this work force and utilise the human resources and accelerate their economic growth.

Planners and policy makers in developing countries like India have to take into account the ongoing demographic changes (number and age structure of the population) so that available human resources are optimally utilised as agents of change and development to achieve improvement in quality of life.

5.3. Demographic Transition in India

Over the last four decades there has been rapid fall in Crude Death Rate (CDR) from 25.1 in 1951 to 9.8 in 1991 and less steep decline in the Crude Birth Rate (CBR) from 40.8 in 1951 to 29.5 in 1991. The annual exponential population growth rate has been over 2% in the period 1961-90. During the nineties the decline in CBR has been steeper than that in the (CDR) and consequently, the annual population growth rate has fallen below 2%. The rate of decline in population growth is likely to be further accelerated during the next decade. The changes in the population growth rates have been relatively slow, steady and sustained. As a result the country was able to achieve a relatively gradual change in the population numbers and age structure. The short and long term adverse consequences of too rapid decline in birth rates and change in age structure on the social and economic development were avoided and the country was able to adapt to these changes without massive disruptions of developmental efforts. In spite of the uniform national norms set under the 100% Centrally Funded and Centrally Sponsored Scheme (CSS) of Family Welfare, there are substantial differences in the performance between States as assessed by IMR and CBR. Though the decline in CBR and IMR has occurred in all States, the rate of decline is slower in some States.

5.3.1. Consequences of Population Growth

5.3.1.1. Environmental and ecological consequences

The already densely populated developing countries contribute to over 95% of the population growth and rapid population growth could lead to environmental deterioration. Developed countries are less densely populated and contribute very little to population growth; however, they cause massive ecological damage by the wasteful, unnecessary and unbalanced consumption the consequences of which could adversely affect both the developed and the developing countries.

In many developing countries continued population growth has resulted in pressure on land, fragmentation of land holding, collapsing fisheries, shrinking forests, rising temperatures, loss of plant and animal species. Global warming due to increasing use of fossil fuels (mainly by the developed countries) could have serious effects on the populous coastal regions in developing countries, their food production and essential water supplies. The Intergovernmental Panel on Climate Change has projected that, if current greenhouse gas emission trends continue, the mean global surface temperature will rise from 1 to 3.5 degrees Celsius in the next century. The panel's best estimate scenario projects a sea-level rise of 15 to 95 centimeters by 2100. The ecological impact of rising oceans would include increased flooding, coastal erosion, salination of aquifers and coastal cropland and displacement of millions of people living near the coast. Patterns of precipitation are also likely to change, which combined with increased average temperatures, could substantially alter the relative agricultural productivity of different regions. Greenhouse gas emissions are closely linked to both population growth and development.

Slower population growth in developing countries and ecologically sustainable lifestyles in developed countries would make reduction in green house gas emission easier to achieve and provide more time and options for adaptation to climate change. Rapid population growth, developmental activities either to meet the growing population or the growing needs of the population as well as changing lifestyles and consumption patterns pose major challenge to preservation and promotion of ecological balance in India.

Population growth, rising income levels, changing technologies, increasing consumption pattern will all have adverse impact on environment. Ensuring that there is no further deterioration depends on choices made by the population about family size, life styles, environmental protection and equity. Availability of appropriate technology and commitment towards ensuring sustainable development is increasing throughout the world. Because of these, it might be possible to initiate steps to see that the natural carrying capacity of the environment is not damaged beyond recovery and ecological balance is to a large extent maintained. It is imperative that the environmental sustainability of all developmental projects is taken care of by appropriate inputs at the planning, implementation, monitoring and evaluation stages.

5.3.1.2. Urbanisation

The proportion of people in developing countries who live in cities has almost doubled since 1960 (from less than 22 per cent to more than 40 per cent), while in more developed regions the urban share has grown from 61 per cent to 76 per cent. Urbanisation is projected to continue well into the next century. By 2030, it is expected that nearly 5 billion (61 per cent) of the world's 8.1 billion people will live in cities. India shares this global trend toward urbanisation. Globally, the number of cities with 10 million or more inhabitants is increasing rapidly, and most of these new "megacities" are in developing regions. In 1960, only New York and Tokyo had more than 10 million people.

Like many other demographic changes, urbanisation has both positive and negative effects. Cities and towns have become the engines of social change and rapid economic development. Urbanisation is associated with improved access to education, employment, health care; these result in increase in age at marriage, reduction in family size and improvement in health indices. As people have moved towards and into cities, information has flowed outward. Better communication and transportation now link urban and rural areas both economically and socially creating an urban-rural continuum of communities with improvement in some aspects of lifestyle of both.

The ever-increasing reach of mass media communicates new ideas, points of reference, and available options are becoming more widely recognised, appreciated and sought. This phenomenon has affected health care, including reproductive health, in many ways. For instance, radio and television programmes that discuss gender equity, family size preference and family planning options are now reaching formerly isolated rural populations. This can create demand for services for mothers and children, higher contraceptive use, and fewer unwanted pregnancies, smaller healthier families and lead to more rapid population stabilisation.

But the rapid growth of urban population also poses some serious challenges. Urban population growth has outpaced the development of basic minimum services; housing, water supply, sewerage and solid waste disposal are far from adequate; increasing waste generation at home, offices and industries, coupled with poor waste disposal facilities result in rapid environmental deterioration. Increasing automobiles add to air pollution. All these have adverse effect on ecology and health. Poverty persists in urban and peri-urban areas; awareness about the glaring inequities in close urban setting may lead to social unrest.

5.3.1.3. Development of rural population

Over seventy per cent of India's population still lives in rural areas. There are substantial differences between the states in the proportion of rural and urban population (varying from almost 90 per cent in Assam and Bihar to 61 per cent in Maharashtra). Agriculture is the largest and one of the most important sector of the rural economy and contributes both to economic growth and employment. Its contribution to the Gross Domestic Product has declined over the last five decades but agriculture still remains the source of livelihood for over 70 per cent of the country's population. A large proportion of the rural work force is small and consists of marginal farmers and landless agricultural labourers. There is substantial under employment among these people; both wages and productivity are low. These in turn result in poverty; it is estimated that 320 million people are still living below the poverty line in rural India.

Though poverty has declined over the last three decades, the number of rural poor has in fact increased due to the population growth. Poor tend to have larger families, which puts enormous burden on their meager resources, and prevent them from breaking out of the shackles of poverty. In States like Tamil Nadu where replacement level of fertility has been attained, population growth rates are much lower than in many other States; but the population density is high and so there is a pressure on land. In States like Rajasthan, Uttar Pradesh, Bihar and Madhya Pradesh population is growing rapidly, resulting in increasing pressure on land and resulting land fragmentation. Low productivity of small landholders leads to poverty, low energy intake and under nutrition, and this, in turn, prevents the development thus creating a vicious circle. In most of the states non-farm employment in rural areas has not grown very much and cannot absorb the growing labour force. Those who are getting educated specially beyond the primary level, may not wish to do manual agricultural work. They would like better opportunities and more remunerative employment. In this context, it is imperative that programmes for skill development, vocational training and technical education are taken up on a large scale in order to generate productive employment in rural areas. The entire gamut of existing poverty alleviation and employment generation programmes may have to be restructured to meet the newly emerging types of demand for employment.

Rural poor have inadequate access to basic minimum services, because of poor connectivity, lack of awareness, inadequate and poorly functional infrastructure. There are ongoing efforts to improve these, but with the growing aspirations of the younger, educated population these efforts may prove to be inadequate to meet the increasing needs both in terms of type and quality of services. Greater education, awareness and better standard of living among the growing younger age group population would create the required consciousness among them that smaller families are desirable; if all the felt needs for health and family welfare services are fully met, it will be possible to enable them to attain their reproductive goals, achieve substantial decline in the family size and improve quality of life.

5.3.1.4. Water supply

In many parts of developed and developing world, water demand substantially exceeds sustainable water supply. It is estimated that currently 430 millions (8% of the global population) are living in countries affected by water stress; by 2020 about one fourth of the global population may be facing chronic and recurring shortage of fresh water. In India, water withdrawal is estimated to be twice the rate of aquifer recharge; as a result water tables are falling by one to three meters every year; tapping deeper aquifers have resulted in larger population groups being exposed to newer health hazards such as high fluoride or arsenic content in drinking water. At the other end of the spectrum, excessive use of water has led to water logging and increasing salinity in some parts of the country. Eventually, both lack of water and water logging could have adverse impact on India's food production. There is very little arable agricultural land, which remains unexploited and in many areas, agricultural technology improvement may not be able to ensure further increase in yield per hectare. It is, therefore, imperative that research in biotechnology for improving development of food grains strains that would tolerate salinity and those which would require less water gets high priority. Simultaneously, a movement towards making water harvesting, storage and its need based use part of every citizens life should be taken up.

5.3.1.5. Food security

Technological innovations in agriculture and increase in area under cultivation have ensured that so far, food production has kept pace with the population growth. Evolution of global and national food security systems has improved access to food. It is estimated that the global population will grow to 9 billion by 2050 and the food production will double; improvement in purchasing power and changing dietary habits (shift to animal products) may further add to the requirement of food grains. Thus, in the next five decades, the food and nutrition security could become critical in many parts of the world especially in the developing countries and pockets of poverty in the developed countries.

In India one of the major achievements in the last fifty years has been the green revolution and self-sufficiency in food production. Over years the coarse grain production has remained stagnant and per capita availability of coarse grain has under gone substantial reduction; there has been a shift away from coarse grains to rice and wheat consumption even among poorer segment of population. One of the benefits of this change is virtual elimination of pellagra, which was widely prevalent among low-income group population in Deccan Plateau whose staple food was sorghum. Coarse grains are less expensive than rice and wheat; they can thus provide higher calories for the same cost as compared to rice and wheat. Coarse grains which are locally produced and procured if made available through TPDS at subsidised rate, may not only substantially bring down the subsidy cost without any reduction in calories provided but also improve "targetting" - as only the most needy are likely to access these coarse grains.

Another area of concern is the lack of sufficient focus and thrust in horticulture; because of this, availability of vegetables especially green leafy vegetables and yellow/red vegetables throughout the year at affordable cost both in urban and rural areas has remained an unfulfilled dream. Health and nutrition education emphasising the importance of consuming these inexpensive rich sources of micronutrients will not result in any change in food habits unless there is harnessing and effective management of horticultural resources in the country to meet the growing needs of the people at affordable cost. States like Tamil Nadu and Himachal Pradesh have initiated some efforts in this direction; similar efforts need be taken up in other states also.

5.3.1.6. Nutrition

At the time of independence the country faced two major nutritional problems; one was the threat of famine and acute starvation due to low agricultural production and lack of appropriate food distribution system. The other was chronic energy deficiency due to poverty, low-literacy, poor access to safe-drinking water, sanitation and health care; these factors led to wide spread prevalence of infections and ill health in children and adults. Kwashiorkor, marasmus, goitre, beri beri, blindness due to Vitamin-A deficiency and anaemia were major public health problems. The country adopted multi-sectoral, multi-pronged strategy to combat the major nutritional problems and to improve nutritional status of the population.

During the last 50 years considerable progress has been achieved. Famines no longer stalk the country. There has been substantial reduction in moderate and severe under nutrition in children and some improvement in nutritional status of all segments of population. Kwashiorkor, marasmus, pellagra, lathyrism, beri beri and blindness due to severe Vitamin-A deficiency have become rare. However, it is a matter of concern that milder forms of Chronic Energy Deficiency (CED) and micronutrient deficiencies continue to be widely prevalent in adults and children. In view of the fact that population growth in India will continue for the next few decades, it is essential that appropriate strategies are devised to improve food and nutrition security of families, identify individuals/families with severe forms of CED and provide them assistance to over come these problem.

5.3.2. Implications of Population Projections

Right from 1958 the Planning Commission has been constituting an Expert Group on Population Projections prior to the preparation of each of the Five Year Plans so that the information on the population status at the time of initiation of the Plan and population projections for future are available during the preparation of the Plan. Population projections have been utilised not only for planning to ensure provision of essentials necessities such as food, shelter and clothing but also prerequisites for human development such as education, employment and health care. Over the years there has been considerable refinement in the methodology used for population projections and substantial improvement in the accuracy of predictions.

5.3.2.1. Economic implications

Population growth and its relation to economic growth has been a matter of debate for over a century. The early Malthusian view was that population growth is likely to impede economic growth because it will put pressure on the available resources, result in reduction in per capita income and resources; this, in turn, will result in deterioration in quality of life. Contrary to the Malthusian predictions, several of the East Asian countries have been able to achieve economic prosperity and improvement in quality of life in spite of population growth. This has been attributed to the increase in productivity due to development and utilisation of innovative technologies by the young educated population who formed the majority of the growing population. These countries have been able to exploit the dynamics of demographic transition to achieve economic growth by using the human resources as the engine driving the economic development; improved employment with adequate emoluments has promoted saving and investment which in turn stimulated economic growth. However, not all countries, which have undergone demographic transition, have been able to transform their economies.

Sri Lanka in South Asia underwent demographic transition at the same time as South East Asian countries but has not achieved the economic transition. It is now realised that population growth or demographic transition can have favourable impact on economic growth only when there are optimal interventions aimed at human resource development (HRD) and appropriate utilisation of available human resources. For India the current phase of demographic transition with low dependency ratio and high working age group population, represents both a challenge and an opportunity. The challenge is to develop these human resources through appropriate education and skill development and utilise them fully by giving them appropriate jobs with adequate emoluments; if this challenge is met through well planned schemes for HRD and employment generation which are implemented effectively, there will be improved national productivity and personal savings rates; appropriate investment of these savings will help the country to achieve the economic transition from low economic growth - low per capita income to high economic growth - high per capita income. It is imperative to make the best use of this opportunity so as to enable the country and its citizens to vault to the high income- high economic growth status and stabilise at that level.

5.3.2.2. Interstate differences

There are marked differences between States in size of the population and population growth rates, the time by which replacement level of fertility is to be achieved and age structure of the population. If the present trend continues, most of the Southern and the Western States are likely to achieve TFR of 2.1 by 2010. Urgent energetic steps to assess and fully meet the unmet needs for maternal and child health (MCH) care and contraception through improvement in availability and access to family welfare services are needed in the States of UP, MP, Rajasthan and Bihar in order to achieve a faster decline in their mortality and fertility rates. In all the states performance in the social and economic sector has been poor. The poor performance is the outcome of poverty, lliteracy and poor development, which co-exist and reinforce each other. The quality and coverage under health services is poor and the unmet need for FW services is about 30%. Urgent energetic steps are required to be initiated to assess and fully meet the unmet needs for maternal and child health (MCH) care and contraception through improvement in availability and access to family welfare services in the states of UP, MP, Rajasthan and Bihar in order to achieve a faster decline in their mortality and fertility rates. The performance of these states would determine the year and size of the population at which the country achieves population stabilisation.

There are also marked differences between States in socio-economic development. Increasing investments and rapid economic development are likely to occur in the States where literacy rates are high; there is ready availability of skilled work force and adequate infrastructure. In these States, population growth rates are low. If equitable distribution of the income and benefits generated by development is ensured, substantial increase in per capita income and improvement in quality of life could occur in these States in a relatively short time.

In majority of States with high population growth rates, the performance in the social and economic sector has been poor. The poor performance could be the outcome of a variety of factors including paucity of natural, financial or human resources. Poverty, illiteracy and poor development co-exist and aggravate each other. In order to promote equity and reduce disparity between States, special assistance has been provided to the poorly performing States.

The higher population growth rates and low per capita income in poorly performing States are likely to have a major impact on several social sector programmes. The health status of the population in these States is poor; the health sector programme will require inputs not only for improving infrastructure and manpower, but also increasing efficiency and improving performance. The Family Welfare Programme has to address the massive task of meeting all the unmet needs for MCH and contraception so that there is a rapid decline in mortality and fertility rates. Due to high birth rate, the number of children requiring schooling will be large. The emphasis in the education sector on primary education is essential to ensure that the resource constraints do not result in an increase in either proportion or number of illiterates. Emphasis on prevocational and vocational training in schools will enable these children to acquire skills through which they will find gainful employment later.

5.3.2.3. Migration

The available data from census shows that until 1991 both internal and international migration has been negligible. The Technical Group while computing the population projection upto 2016, has assumed that the component of migration between major States and from India will be negligible. This assumption may not be valid if there is further widening of the disparity between States in terms of economic growth and employment opportunity. Given the combination of high population growth, low literacy and lack of employment opportunities in the poorly performing States, there may be increasing rural to urban migration as well as interstate migration especially of unskilled workers. Such migration may in the short run assist the migrants in overcoming economic problems associated with unemployment. However, the migrant workers and their families may face problems in securing shelter, education and health care. It is essential to build up a mechanism for monitoring these changes. Steps will have to be taken to provide for the minimum essential needs of the vulnerable migrant population.

5.3.2.4. Labour, employment and manpower

Population, which is engaged in any economic activity (employed persons) and population seeking work (unemployed) constitute Labour Force. India has the second largest labour force in the world. Projection of labour force is pre-requisite ensuring optimal utilisation of available human resources. Manpower development is then taken up to provide adequate labour force, of appropriate skills and quality to different sectors so that there is rapid socioeconomic development and there is no mismatch between skills required and skills available. Planning also attempts to provide enabling environment for employment generation (both self employment and wage employment) in public, private and voluntary sectors in urban and rural areas.

5.3.2.5. Labour force

Labour force in India will be increasing by more than 10 million per annum during 1997-2012. It will be imperative to plan for and achieve adequate agricultural and industrial growth to absorb this work force. Most of the persons entering the labour force will be educated and have some skills. Increasing literacy and decreasing birth rates may result in more women seeking economically productive work outside home. It will be important to generate appropriate and renumerative employment at places where labour force are available so as to reduce interstate and urban migration in search of employment. Attempts should be made to eliminate bonded labour, employment of children and women in hazardous industries and minimising occupational health hazards.

Planners face the challenge to have sustained high economic growth rate in sectors that are labour-intensive to ensure adequate employment generation for productively utilising this massive work force. If the massive work force of literate, skilled, aware men and women in age-group 20-60 years get fully employed and adequately paid they could trigger off a period of rapid economic development. As they have very few dependant children and elders there will be increased savings and investments at household level; this in turn will improve the availability of resources for accelerating economic growth. The current stage of demographic transition thus provides the country with the opportunity window for using human resources as the engine to power economic development and improving the quality of life of all the citizens.

5.3.2.6. Sex ratio

The reported decline in the sex ratio during the current century has been a cause for concern. The factors responsible for this continued decline are as yet not clearly identified. However, it is well recognised that the adverse sex ratio is a reflection of the gender disparity. Higher childhood mortality in girl children is yet another facet of the existing gender disparities and consequent adverse effect on survival. In the reproductive age group the mortality rates among women are higher than those among men. The continued high maternal mortality is one of the major factors responsible for this. Effective implementation of the Reproductive and Child Health Programme is expected to result in a substantial reduction in maternal mortality.

At the moment, the longevity at birth among women is only marginally higher than that among men. However over the next decade life expectancy among women will progressively increase. Once the reproductive age group is crossed, the mortality rates among women are lower as women outlive and outnumber men in the age group 65 and above. The needs especially of the widowed women have to be met so that quality of life does not deteriorate. The census 2001 will collect and report vital data on sex disaggregated basis; this will be of help in identifying and taking up appropriate interventions in correcting gender disparity; continued collection, collation, analysis and reporting of sex disaggregated data from all social sectors will also provide a mechanism to monitor whether girls and women have equal access to services.

5.3.2.7. Increasing longevity

Over the coming decades the country will be facing a progressive increase both in the proportion and number of persons beyond 60 years of age. Over the next 20 years the population of more than 60 years will grow form 62.3 million to 112.9 million; the subsequent decades will witness massive increase in this age group. Increasing longevity will inevitably bring in its wake increase in the prevalence of non-communicable diseases. The growing number of senior citizens in the country poses a major challenge and the cost of providing socio-economic security and health care to this population has to be met. Currently several region and culture specific innovative interventions to provide needed care to this population are underway; among these are efforts to reverse the trend of break up of joint families. If these efforts succeed, it will be possible to provide necessary care for rapidly increasing population of senior citizens in the subsequent two decades within the resources of the family and the country.

Majority of the people in their sixties will be physically and psychologically fit and would like to participate both in economic and social activities. They should be encouraged and supported to lead a productive life and contribute to the national development. Senior citizens in their seventies and beyond and those with health problems would require assistance. So far, the families have borne major share in caring for the elderly. This will remain the ideal method; however, there are growing number of elderly without family support; for them, alternate modes for caring may have to be evolved and implemented. Improved health care has "added years to life". The social sectors have to make the necessary provisions for improving the quality of life of these senior citizens so that they truly "add life to years."

5.3.2.8. Health implication

Population growth during demographic transition will lead to overcrowding, poverty, undernutrition, environmental deterioration, poor quality of life and increase in disease burden. Experience in the last few decades has shown that this may not always be correct. India is currently in the phase of demographic transition when the increase in population is mainly among younger, better educated and healthy population with low morbidity and mortality rate. The challenge for the health sector is to promote healthy life styles, improve access to and utilisation of health care so that the country can achieve substantial reduction in mortality and morbidity. Occupational health and environmental health programme need be augmented to ensure that working population remain healthy and productive. If these challenges are fully met, it is possible to accelerate reduction in morbidity and mortality rate in this age group and improve health indices of the country.

With growing number of senior citizens there may be substantial increase in health care needs especially for management of non-communicable diseases. Increasing availability and awareness about technological advances for management of these problems, rising expectations of the population and the ever escalating cost of health care are some of the problems that the health care system has to cope with. Health care delivery systems will have to gear up to taking up necessary preventive, promotive, curative and rehabilitative care for growing population of senior citizens.

5.3.3. Family Welfare Programme

India, the second most populous country in the world, has no more than 2.5% of global land but is the home of 1/6th of the world's population. The prevailing high maternal, infant, childhood morbidity and mortality, low life expectancy and high fertility and associated high morbidity had been a source of concern for public health professionals right from the pre-independence period. The Bhore Committee Report (1946), which laid the foundation for health service planning in India, gave high priority to provision of maternal and child health services and improving their nutritional and health status. It is noteworthy that this report which emphasised the importance of providing integrated preventive, promotive and curative primary health care services preceded the Alma Ata declaration by over three decades. Under the Constitution of India elimination of poverty, ignorance and ill health are three important goals.

In 1951, the infant republic took stock of the existing situation in the country and initiated the first Five Year Development Plan. Living in a resource poor country with high population density, the Planners recognised in the census figures of 1951, the potential threat posed by population explosion and the need to take steps to avert it. It was recognised that population stabilisation is an essential prerequisite for sustainability of development process so that the benefits of economic development result in enhancement of the well being of the people and improvement in quality of life. India became the first country in the world to formulate a National Family Planning Programme in 1952, with the objective of "reducing birth rate to the extent necessary to stabilise the population at a level consistent with requirement of national economy". Thus, the key elements of health care to women and children and provision of contraceptive services have been the focus of India's health services right from the time of India's independence. Successive Five Year Plans have been providing the policy framework and funding for planned development of nationwide health care infrastructure and manpower. The Centrally Sponsored and 100% centrally funded Family Welfare Programme provides additional infrastructure, manpower and drugs, vaccines contraceptives and other consumables needed for improving health status of women and children and to meet all the felt needs for fertility regulation.

The National Family Health Survey (NFHS) 1992-93 had provided an independent nation wide evaluation of the progress and problems in delivery of Family Welfare services in the country. The survey confirmed that in spite of obvious constraints and inadequacies, the governmental network can, and does, provides most of the MCH and contraceptive care.

There is a popular belief that the population growth is due to poor performance in the health sector. This is not correct. The population growth that the country (and the world) had witnessed in the last five decades is mainly because of rapid reduction in the death rates due to health care and is inevitable during the frist three phases of demographic transition. India's progress in demographic transition has been a slow but sustained; unlike some other developing countries India's population growth never exceeded 2.2% even at its peak; the decline in population growth once started has been sustained. This orderly progression has been achieved through improving access to family welfare services and ensuring peoples participation. Concern has been expressed by some groups that the RCH programme which essentially aims at improving quality and coverage of the already ongoing maternal and child health and contraceptive care may not be successful in accelerating the decline in fertility and help the country to achieve rapid population stabilisation and that there is a need for new path breaking innovations. Ongoing evaluations, however, do not suggest that there is a need for change in policy, strategy and programme content; all these studies have emphasised that there is a huge unmet need for services and there is an urgent need to improve access to good quality services to meet this need, the focus of the RCH initiative is on this task.

5.4. Conclusion

Demographic transition is a global phenomenon; population growth is inevitable in the initial phases of the transition. For India the current phase of the demographic transition is both a challenge and an opportunity. The challenge is to ensure human development and optimum utilisation of human resources. The opportunity is to utilise available human resources to achieve rapid economic development and improvement in quality of life. Over the last five decades the country has built up a massive healthcare infrastructure for delivery of FW services to the population in the Govt, private and voluntary sectors. The RCH programme envisages wider range of services and improvement in quality of services provided. There is universal awareness about the need for these services. In the next two decades the population growth will be mainly among the young adults who will be more literate, aware and likely to make optimal use of available facilities. India is currently in the phase of demographic transition during which where it will be possible for the country to accelerate the pace of decline in fertility. If the population now has ready access to good quality services at affordable cost, it will be possible for them to meet all their needs, achieve the desired family size and enable the country to achieve population stabilsation rapidly.

Demographic transition does not occur in isolation. Simultaneously, there are ongoing economic transition, education transition, health transition and reproductive health transition. All these affect human development. If there is synergy between these transitions; the transitions can be completed rapidly; there will be substantial improvement in human development and economic development. The focus of planners, programme implementers and the people during the next two decades will have to be in achieving the synergy so that India can achieve rapid population stabilisation, improvement in economic social and human development.

References

Larry Hobbs, "Complexity of factors involved in human population growth", *Environmental Health Perspectives*, Sept 2004.

Salmony S.E., "Food and population growth", *Environmental Health Perspectives,* 112:A339-A340, 2004.

Weinhold B., "Infectious disease: the human cost of our environmental errors, *Environmental Health Perspectives*, 112:A32-A39, 2004.

CHAPTER 6

Determinants of Population Growth

6.1. Introduction

With the persistent increase of the human population- now exceeding six billion-all species face increased pressure on resources. Understanding the factors responsible for limiting populations or causing species' extinctions therefore has increased urgency. Recent developments in population analysis, described below, have refined the understanding of the determinants of population growth rate and linked the theory to field data, and there is increasing interest in applying methods of this kind in conservation, wildlife management and ecotoxicology.

Population growth rate is the summary parameter of trends in population density or abundance. It tells whether density and abundance are increasing, stable or decreasing, and how fast they are changing. Population growth rate describes the per capita rate of growth of a population, either as the factor by which population size increases per year, conventionally given the symbol, l (N_{t+1} / N_t), or as $r = \log_e$l. Generally here, population growth rate will refer to *r*. l is referred to variously as 'finite growth rate', 'finite rate of increase', 'net reproductive rate' or 'population multiplication rate'. *r* is known as 'rate of natural increase', 'instantaneous growth rate', 'exponential rate of increase' or 'fitness'. In the simplest population model all individuals in the population are assumed equivalent, with the same death rates and birth rates, and there is no migration in or out of the population, so exponential growth occurs; in this model, population growth rate =*r*= instantaneous birth rate instantaneous death rate.

Population growth rate is typically estimated using either census data over time or from demographic data. Census data are analysed by the linear regression of the natural logarithms of abundance over time, and demographic data using the Euler-Lotka equation and population projection matrices. The two methods of estimation can give similar values, as shown in studies of the northern spotted owl,

Strix occidentalis caurina, greater amingo, Phoenicopterus ruber roseus, and pea aphids, Acyrthosiphon pisum.

The census method has greater statistical power to detect a population decline than the demographic method when applied to high-density populations and the reverse occurs with low-density populations. The estimation of the finite population growth rate (l) may be biased by several factors: the manner of analysing census data with zeros, by the existence of spatial variance and spatial-temporal covariance, and by the scale of the area studied. r varies from a minimum value of 2 to a value of 0.0 for a stable population, to a maximum value (rm ax) when the population increases at the maximum possible rate, when food is abundant and there are no predators, pathogens and competitors. The corresponding values of l are 0.0, 1.0 and l max. The frequency distribution of l of a population persisting through time and space is positively skewed, with the maximum value further to the right of the mode than the minimum value. The frequency distribution of r is generally closer to a normal distribution.

6.2. Projection of Future Population Sizes

The importance of population growth rate is that it allows qualified projection of future population sizes. If there were no density dependence then population growth would be exponential, at a rate calculable from the Euler-Lotka equation using demographic data from the existing population. If the form of density dependence were constant and known, then the future population dynamics could to some degree be predicted. To what extent this can be realised in practice is discussed below; here we wish only to emphasise the central role of population growth rate in the projection of future population sizes.

Density dependence is seen as providing an explicit negative feedback mechanism which regulates the population. When density is below carrying capacity, population growth rate is positive and the population increases towards carrying capacity; conversely when density is above carrying capacity, population growth rate is negative and the population declines. In this way population density is controlled by the mechanism of the negative density dependence of population growth rate, and in the absence of environmental changes or time lags, population density remains in the vicinity of carrying capacity.

6.2.1. Historical Background

The pivotal importance of population growth rate has been recognised for a long time. The idea of geometric population growth restrained at higher densities by the carrying capacity of the environment was put forward in a book by Botero, and was famously elaborated and brought to general attention by Malthus. Detailed interest in tables of mortality began in the late seventeenth century, with mathematical analyses by Huygens and later Buffon among others. Interestingly, Cole suggests that Newton notably 'failed to grasp the basic concept that life expectancy is a function of age.' The proposal that population growth rate declines linearly with population density, known as the logistic equation, was put forward by Verhulst. Population growth rate is central to the work of the modern founding fathers of ecology, but the complexities of its dependence on age-specific birth and death rates have until recently prevented thorough examination of the role of population growth rate. With the advent of modern computing and the development of matrix methods for the analysis of life tables, the importance of population growth rate in the study of population ecology is becoming more widely appreciated.

6.3. Environmental Stress

Environmental stressors can be defined as factors that, when first applied to a population, reduce population growth rate. Examples of stressors may be climatic conditions, toxicants, food quality, pathogens and so on. The advantages of explicit operational definitions of the terms 'stress' and 'stressor' are obvious, and it is encouraging that identical definitions are now used from the population level down to that of molecular responses.

6.4. Population Density

Environmental stressors have negative effects on population growth rate, and the same is true of population density. Indeed the nature of the negative relationship between population density and population growth rate is at the heart of population ecology. If the relationship is linear, the describing equation is the logistic, and many theoretical analyses are built on this assumption. Fowler has argued on theoretical and some empirical grounds that relationships between population growth rate and density are expected to be concave for species with life histories like those of insects, convex for large mammals and similar species, and linear for intermediate species. Concave and convex correspond to values less or greater than one respectively for the shape parameter u in the generalised logistic equation.

Given its fundamental importance in population ecology, it is surprising that data on the form of the dependence of population growth rate on density have only rarely been plotted out and analysed, though Berryman and Turchin give examples. This is partly because the relationship cannot be seen without adequate variation in density in a fairly constant environment; thus the best evidence may come from population recoveries after experimental perturbations. Although a priori density dependence can be expected in real populations that persist long term, recognising the operation of density dependence in real datasets has been the subject of much controversy.

The general conclusion of these meta-analyses is that the existence of density dependence can be established from census data provided sufficient data are available. The objective in analysing density dependence should therefore be the discovery of the form of density dependence, and the effect, if any, of time lags. Despite the successes of the meta-analyses, worries remain about the effects of measurement errors and of fluctuations in environmental variables. None of the existing methods allows for the effects of measurement errors, which may exaggerate the effects of density dependence, and could produce the illusion of density dependence in invariant populations. Some

6.5. Determinants of Population Growth Rate

Because so many factors affect population growth rate, it is never going to be easy to separate their effects when they operate simultaneously. Ecologists have used a variety of methods to study the combined and relative effects on population growth rate of determining factors.

The three main approaches that have been used to identify the determinants of population are the 'density paradigm', the 'demographic paradigm' and the 'mechanistic paradigm.' These are best understood as different simplifications of a rather complicated reality. Intuitively it is clear that population growth rate is fully determined by the complete record of age-specific birth and death rates, and mathematically the link is made by the Euler- Lotka equation. Exploration of the link between population growth rate and the age-specific life table gives the demographic paradigm. Age-specific birth and death rates depend causally on such factors as food supply per individual, parasite burdens, predation, environmental stressors and interference competition, and some of these depend directly or indirectly on population density.

Population growth rate gives the mechanistic paradigm, and focusing on the link between population growth rate and population density gives the density paradigm; these two paradigms were identified and contrasted by Krebs. Any or all of these approaches can be undertaken using observational, experimental and modelling studies.

6.5.1. Demographic Paradigm

The demographic paradigm focuses on the relationship between population growth rate and age-specific fecundity and survival. Population growth rate is increased by an increase in fecundity or survival, or by breeding earlier. Detailed examination of the link between population growth rate and demographic parameters is often made using population projection matrices as described by Caswell, although other methods are also available employing the classical Euler-Lotka equation. Because stable age structure is necessary to the derivation of this equation it is often supposed that population growth rate cannot be estimated without stable age structure.

Elasticity analysis is used alongside observation of actual levels of variation in demographic parameters to determine which demographic factors have most effect on population growth rate. In a similar vein Sibly & Smith have argued that traditional 'key factor' analysis should be redesigned to identify the life-history trait whose variation has most effect on population growth rate. Spatial elements have also been incorporated into efforts to explain variation in population growth rate. The contributions to population growth rate of in situ recruitment, survival and immigration can be estimated from mark-recapture studies, as described for meadow voles by Nichols et al. Populations for which emigration exceeds immigration are referred to as source populations.

6.5.2. Mechanistic Paradigm

The mechanistic paradigm focuses on the relationship between population growth rate and variables such as climate, food availability, predator abundance, pathogens and parasites, and competitors. Turchin provides an excellent discussion of what can be treated as variables: ideally one might keep track of the fates of all relevant individuals, but apart from the impossibility of this, there is often more heuristic value in using summary variables such as 'numbers in each age class' and so on. Historically, the mechanistic paradigm was followed in early models of the effects of competition by Lotka and Volterra in the 1920s, of predation, and of pathogens. Monod considered the relationship between population growth rate and resource availability in populations of bacteria, and in an influential experiment Tilman et al. related population growth rate of the diatom Asterionella formosa to the availability of silicon, which diatoms need to secrete their silicate 'shells'. Later, in a theoretical synthesis, Tilman considered more generally the relationship between population growth rate and the availability of resources. These ideas are very similar to the formulations of ecological niche theory and stressors discussed earlier. In the simplest case, the effect of population density on population growth rate is replaced, in the mechanistic paradigm, by resource availability.

If the population is food limited, it may be more appropriate to divide the population food supply by population density. A positive linear relationship between the annual percentage population growth of a barn owl population and abundance of voles, their main food, was reported by Taylor. Stronger inferences of cause and effect can be obtained using experiments. The effects on population dynamics of extrinsic factors have been studied in field-based experiments, such as adding food or removing predators. The more recent emphasis on biological mechanisms has shed new light on population dynamics.

6.6. Analyses of Demography

Density and demography are linked in studies of density dependence operating on mortality, survival or fecundity; k-value analyses fall into this category as k-values are measures of mortality rates. Density dependence of fecundity is studied within k-value analysis by positing a maximum possible fecundity, and treating observed fecundities as falling short in consequence of 'mortality'. This manoeuvre, while awkward, is of course realistic in the case of abortions. There would seem no reason nowadays not to examine the relationships between life-history traits, density and population growth rate directly. This shows how changes in density (dx) which change life-history traits (e.g. dm) result in changes in population growth rate (dr). In practice, dm/dx would be measured as the regression coefficient in, for example, a k-value analysis. The contribution this makes to changing population growth rate is given by the sensitivity of population growth rate to the life-history trait. Formulae for sensitivities are available for many life histories, calculated by implicit differentiation of appropriate forms of the Euler-Lotka equation. Alternatively, the effect of density on population growth rate acting through demographic parameters can be described in density-dependent Leslie matrix models.

The life-history stages at which density-dependent effects occur in mammals were reviewed by Sinclair. Density was found to affect fecundity in over half the large terrestrial herbivores and large marine mammals, and in some species had effects in the early juvenile phase. By contrast, in small mammals and carnivores the effects of density were felt most in the late juvenile phase. Demography and density have been linked for whitetailed deer in the modified logistic equations of Hobbs et al., which assume positive effects of survival and fecundity on finite population growth rate (l) and a linear negative effect of density on recruitment.

Demography and density are used in population viability analyses to model the probable dynamics of small populations. In one implementation, in the software programme Vortex, there is the option to make the demographic parameters density dependent, and outputs include population growth rate and estimated mean time to extinction. Vortex has been used to assess the feasibility of reintroducing wild boar to Scotland.

6.6.1. Analyses of Demography and Mechanisms

The demographic and mechanistic approaches are linked by showing that demographic parameters are affected by variables from different trophic levels, e.g. food availability. The population growth rate of red fox has been related to separate effects of rainfall on fecundity and on survival. In a barn owl population in southern Scotland, Taylor showed that an increase in vole abundance increased fecundity, decreased adult mortality rate and decreased juvenile mortality. The net effect of increasing food abundance on population growth rate of the owls was positive. The finite population growth rate (l) was estimated from survival and recruitment rates with these demographic rates influenced by climate and/or habitat features.

A full analysis shows the effects of trophic factors and density on demography and hence on population growth rate. For instance the rat, Mastomys natalensis, has dynamics determined by the effects of rainfall on fecundity and the effects of rainfall and density on survival. The population dynamics of the kit fox are determined by demographic rates, which are age structured. Reproductive rates were positively related to food availability, which in turn depended on rainfall. Juvenile mortality was positively density dependent. Soay sheep have population dynamics influenced by demography, which in turn depends on weather conditions and density. The many mathematical models that have been used to describe relationships between population growth rate and demographic parameters, mechanistic and density effects suggest a need for a more detailed comparative evaluation of the fit of the models.

Population growth rate decreased as density increased. Population density alone did not account for all the observed variation, however, because population growth rate was higher at the higher food concentration. This is readily understood because individuals living at higher food availability are expected to grow and reproduce faster, resulting in higher population growth rate. The numerical responses of population growth rate to food availability show that populations declined when food per copepod was low, but increased when food availability was higher. The increase in population growth rate with food supply was not linear, because as food increased, the copepods showed diminishing ability to transform extra food into further population growth. When the relationship is linearised using a log transformation, it appears that while food availability accounts for a great deal of the variation in population growth rate, there is still some unexplained variation.

The population's food supply is shared between its members through a process of resource competition. This is why we assess food availability by 'food per copepod'. The additional negative effects of density on population growth rate of T. battagliai could occur because of interference competition influencing reproductive performance, survival or somatic growth or foraging efficiency. Crowding is known to increase swimming activity in T. Negative effects of population density on population growth rate could occur in nature because of density-dependent effects of predators, parasites, pathogens, inter specific competitors and mutualists, but they were excluded in this experiment. So the negative effects of density, additional to effects through food availability, were caused in this experiment by interference competition.

6.6.2. Ecotoxicology and Human Demography

A better understanding of how to estimate population growth rate, and what determines population growth rate, is fundamental to the application of population growth rate to wildlife management and other topics in population ecology. The three classical applications of conservation, harvesting and pest control aim to increase, maintain and decrease population growth rate, respectively. Each of these applications also affects the frequency distribution of population growth rate. Of general concern in conservation biology is population performance at low density, which is the danger zone for endangered species. Population growth rate may be submaximal when density is low because of the difficulty of finding mates or because of an effect of predation on a prey population, wherein the predator has a type III functional response.

Another potentially important issue in conservation biology is the effect of inbreeding on population growth. Although there is debate about the practical significance of inbreeding in wild animal populations, it is easy to see that it could be important in small isolated populations, because we know from the Euler-Lotka equation that any reductions in fecundity and survival caused by inbreeding would necessarily depress population growth rate. Inbreeding is included as a determinant of population growth rate in population viability analyses such as Vortex. These topics in conservation biology focus on the small population size being a cause of conservation problems.

Another common theme in conservation biology is the decline of populations because of high mortality caused by people. The rate of population growth of populations subject to intensive illegal harvest, such as the African elephant and black rhinoceros has been related to the effort expended in reducing or preventing poaching. The dynamics of seabirds, such as the wandering albatross, are influenced by fishing activities. The rate of population decline depended on the cumulative number of long line fishing hooks set in albatross foraging areas. These studies use the mechanistic approach to identify the causes of population declines.

Also of general interest are the effects of habitat loss, and research here aims to identify the main features of wildlife habitats, and to establish the way they affect distribution and abundance, i.e. to characterise each species' ecological niche. Traditionally such research has involved measuring a large number of habitat features though typically not including food, predators, pathogens and competitors. In an encouraging effort to advance wildlife habitat studies and hence wildlife management in general, Morrison recommended a change to a focus on resources such as food, and their effects on survival and reproduction. Such a focus would be a shift to demographic - mechanistic analysis as described above, and if implemented would lead to greater understanding of mechanisms determining population growth rate.

The sustainable harvest of a wildlife population growing according to logistic growth is a function of abundance, carrying capacity and the maximum rate of population growth. Species at the same abundance having the same carrying capacity have higher sustainable annual harvests if their rm ax values are higher. When rmax is very low, as in long-lived species like whales and elephants, a sustained harvest may not be economic. Variation in the effects of environmental factors lowers the level of sustained harvest and of course increases the variation of the harvest. Negative effects of harvesting on population growth rate have been described in whitetailed deer in Ontario, mallard in North America, and moose in Norway.

Pest control is another field where population growth rate is central; indeed, several early population ecologists studied pests. A pest control programme may become a sustained harvest if pest abundance is reduced and kept at low levels. Pest populations may, however, adapt to control by developing resistance to pesticides. The rate of development of resistance depends on population growth rate and generation interval. Population growth rate can also be seen as the key-unifying concept in ecotoxicology. Thus, pollutants can be defined as environmental chemicals that exceed normal background levels and have the potential to adversely affect birth, growth or mortality rates, with consequent reduction in population growth rate. Pollutants appear as a particular case of environmental stressors. Although the impact of pollutants on organisms is studied within ecotoxicology at different organisational levels, from biochemistry through to communities, each with its own measure of pollutant effect, it can be argued that population growth rate provides the best summary statistic.

Population growth rate is a better measure of responses to toxicants than are individual-level effects, because it integrates potentially complex interactions among life-history traits and provides a more relevant measure of ecological impact. By contrast there are advantages in building up from the level of individual behaviour to a population level perspective on population growth rate. Where complex models of the determinants of population growth rate are used for management purposes, model validation is clearly of crucial importance.

The logistic equation results from human competition for the means of subsistence, namely food, clothing material and fuel. They calculated the carrying capacity of the continental United States as 197 million, but noted that at the levels of production then obtaining it would be necessary to import about half the food supply. Their projections look a little low now, but this can be attributed to technological advances. A recent projection for the global human population based on existing downward trends in fertility indicates that population growth will slow over the coming decades, and peak in ca. 2070 at a population size around nine billion.

6.7. Conclusion

Population growth rate is the unifying variable linking the various facets of population ecology; thus analyses of population regulation, density dependence, resource and interference competition and the effects of environmental stress are all best undertaken with population growth rate as the response variable. Effects of time lags can also, in principle, be treated within this framework. Such analyses are needed not only to improve the quality of the underlying science, but also to increase the realism and accuracy of prediction in key applied areas such as conservation, wildlife management and ecotoxicology.

References

Berryman, A. A., *Principles of population dynamics and their application*, Cheltenham, UK: Stanley Thornes, 1999.

Klemola, T., Korpimaki, E. & Koivula, M., "Rate of population change in voles from different phases of the population cycle", *Oikos,* 2002

Krebs, C. J., *Two paradigms of population regulation*, *Wildl. Res.* **22**, 1–10, 1995

Lutz, W. & Qiang, R., "Determinants of human population growth", *Phil. Trans. R. Soc. Lond.* B **357**,1197–1210, 2002.

Lutz, W., Sanderson, W. & Scherbov, S., "The end of world population growth", *Nature,* 2001.

Malthus, T. R., *An essay on the principle of population*, London: J. Johnson, 1798

Murdoch, W.W., "Population regulation in theory and practice", *Ecology* **75**, 271–287, 1994

CHAPTER 7

Dynamic and Demographic Transition of Population

7.1. Introduction

The transition from stagnation to growth and the associated phenomenon of the great divergence have been the subject of an intensive research in the growth literature in recent years. The inconsistency of exogenous and endogenous neoclassical growth models with some of the most fundamental features of process of development, induced growth theorists to advance a unified growth theory that captures in a single framework the epoch of Malthusian stagnation, the contemporary era of sustained economic growth, and the fundamental driving forces of the recent transition between these distinct regimes.

The understanding of the contemporary growth process is fragile and incomplete unless growth theory would be based on proper micro-foundations that reflect the qualitative aspects of the growth process and its central driving forces over most of human existence. Moreover, a comprehensive understanding of the hurdles faced by less developed economies in reaching a state of sustained economic growth would be futile unless the factors that prompted the transition of the currently developed economies into a state of sustained economic growth would be identified and their implications modified to account for the differences in the growth structure of less developed economies in an interdependent world.

Unified growth theory, first advanced by Galor and Weil, suggests that the transition from stagnation to growth is an inevitable by-product of the inherent Malthusian interaction between population and technology, and its ultimate impact on the demand for human capital and thereby on the onset of the demographic transition. Variations in the timing of the transition across countries and regions reflect initial differences in geographical factors and historical accidents and their manifestation in variations in institutional, demographic, and cultural factors, trade patterns, colonial status, and public policy.

The demographic transition that swept the world in the course of the last century has been identified as one of the prime forces in the movement from an epoch of stagnation to a state of sustained economic growth. It brought about a significant reduction in fertility rates and population growth in various regions of the world, enabling economies to convert a larger share of the fruits of factor accumulation and technological progress into growth of income per capita.

7.2. Evidence from the History

The evolution of economies over most of human history was marked by Malthusian stagnation. Technological progress and population growth were miniscule by modern standards and the average growth rate of income per capita in various regions of the world was even slower due to the offsetting effect of population growth on the expansion of resources per capita. In the past two centuries, in contrast, the pace of technological progress increased significantly in association with the process of industrialisation. Various regions of the world economy departed from the Malthusian trap and initially experienced a considerable rise in the growth rates of income per capita and population. Unlike episodes of technological progress in the pre-Industrial Revolution era that failed to generate sustained economic growth, the increasing role of human capital in the production process in the second phase of the Industrial Revolution ultimately prompted a demographic transition, liberating the gains in productivity from the counterbalancing effects of population growth. The decline in population growth and the associated advancement in technological progress and human capital formation paved the way for the emergence of the modern state of sustained economic growth.

The evolution of population growth in the world economy has been non-monotonic. The growth of world population was sluggish during the Malthusian epoch, creeping at an average annual rate of about 0.1% over the years 0-1820. The Western European take-off along with that of the Western Offshoots brought about a sharp increase in population growth in these regions and consequently in the world as a whole. The annual average rate of population growth in the world increased gradually reaching 0.8% in the years 1870-1913. The delayed take-off. of less developed regions and the significant increase in their income per capita generated a further gradual increase in the rate of population growth in the world, despite the decline in population growth in Western Europe and the Western Offshoots, reaching a high level of 1.92% per year in the period 1950- 1973. Ultimately, however, the onset of the demographic transition in less developed economies in the second half of the 20th century, reduced population growth to an average rate of about 1.63% per year in the 1973-1998 period.

The timing of the demographic transition differed significantly across regions. The reduction in population growth occurred in Western Europe, the Western Offshoots, and Eastern Europe towards the end of the 19th century and in the beginning of the 20th century, whereas Latin America and Asia experienced a decline in the rate of population growth only in the last decades of the 20th century. Africa's population growth, in contrast, has been rising steadily, although this pattern is likely to reverse in the near future due to the decline in total fertility rate in this region since the 1980s.

The mortality decline preceded the decline in fertility rates in a large number of countries in the world, with the notable exceptions of France and the United States. The decline in mortality rates preceded the decline in fertility rates in Western European countries and it began in England nearly 140 years prior to the decline in fertility and in Sweden and Finland approximately 100 years prior to the decline in fertility. The decline in fertility during the demographic transition outpaced the decline in mortality rates and brought about a decline in the number of children who survived to their reproduction age.

7.3. Theories of Demographic Transition

Theories of demographic transition attempt to capture the determinants of the significant reduction in fertility rates and population growth that characterised the world in the past century, enabling economies to convert an increasing share of the benefits of factor accumulation and technological progress into growth of output per capita via a reduction of the dilution of the stock of capital and land, enhancement of investment in the human capital, and changes in the age distribution of the population, temporarily increasing the size of the labour force relative to the population as a whole.

7.3.1. Decline in Infant and Child Mortality

The decline in infant and child mortality rates that preceded the decline in fertility rates in many countries, with the notable exceptions of France and the US, has been demographers' favourite explanation for the onset of the decline in fertility in the course of the demographic transition. Nevertheless, it appears that this viewpoint is inconsistent with historical evidence. While it is highly plausible that mortality rates were among the factors that affected the level of total fertility rates along human history, historical evidence does not lend credence to the argument that the decline in mortality rates accounts for the reversal of the positive historical trend between income and fertility.

The mortality decline in Western Europe started nearly a century prior to the decline in fertility and was associated initially with increasing fertility rates in some countries and non-decreasing fertility rates in other countries. In particular, the decline in mortality started in England in the 1730s and was accompanied by a steady increase in fertility rates until 1820. The significant rise in income per capita in the Post-Malthusian Regime increased the desirable number of surviving offspring and thus, despite the decline in mortality rates, fertility increased significantly so as to reach this higher desirable level of surviving offspring. The decline in fertility during the demographic transition occurred in a period in which this pattern of increased income per capita (and its potential positive e.ect on fertility) was intensified, while the pattern of declining mortality (and its adverse e.ect on fertility) maintained the trend that existed in the 140 years that preceded the demographic transition. Thus in the absence of the intervention of a third factor fertility would have risen further. The reversal in the fertility patterns in England as well as other Western European countries in the 1870s suggests therefore that the demographic transition was prompted by a different universal force than the decline in infant and child mortality.

Furthermore, most relevant from an economic point of view is the cause of the reduction of surviving offspring, that was observed during the demographic transition is unlikely to follow from mortality decline. Mortality decline would have led to a reduction in the number of surviving offspring. There exists a significant precautionary demand for children, i.e., individuals are significantly risk averse with respect to their expected number of surviving offspring and they hold a buffer stock of children in a high mortality environment.

7.3.2. Rise in Income Level Per Capita

The demographic transition was triggered by the rise in income per capita and its asymmetric effects on households income and on the opportunity cost of raising children. Becker advances the argument that the decline in fertility in the course of the demographic transition is a by-product of the rise in income per capita that preceded the demographic transition. He argues that the rise in income induced a fertility decline because the positive income effect on fertility that was generated by the rise in wages was dominated by the negative substitution effect that was brought about by the rising opportunity cost of children. Similarly, he argues that the income elasticity with respect to child quality is greater than that with respect to child quantity, and hence a rise in income led to a decline in fertility along with a rise in the investment in each child.

This theory suggests that the timing of the demographic transition across countries in similar stages of development would reflect differences in income per capita. However, the decline in fertility occurred in the same decade across Western European countries that differed significantly in their income per capita. The simultaneity of the demographic transition across Western European countries that differed significantly in their income per capita suggests that the high level of income that was reached by Western Europeans countries in the Post-Malthusian regime had a very limited role in the demographic transition.

This underlined the critical role of the acceleration in technological progress and its e.ect on the demand for human capital in the demographic transition, despite the large differences in the levels of income per capita across European countries that experiences the demographic transition in the same time period, the growth rates of income per capita of these European countries were rather similar during their demographic transition.

7.3.3. Rise in the Demand for Human Capital

7.3.3.1. Mechanism

The gradual rise in the demand for human capital in the second phase of the Industrial Revolution (and in the process of industrialisation of less developed economies) and its close association with the timing of the demographic transitions, has led researchers to argue that the increasing role of human capital in the production process induced households to increase investment in the human capital of their offspring, ultimately leading to the onset of the demographic transition.

Galor and Weil, argue that the acceleration in the rate of technological progress gradually increased the demand for human capital in the second phase of the Industrial Revolution, inducing parents to invest in the human capital of their offspring. The increase in the rate of technological progress and the associated increase in the demand for human capital brought about two effects on population growth. On the one hand, improved technology eased households' budget constraints and provided more resources for the quality as well as the quantity of children. On the other hand, it induced a reallocation of these increased resources toward child quality. In the early stages of the transition from the Malthusian regime, the effect of technological progress on parental income dominated, and the population growth rate as well as the average quality increased. Ultimately, further increases in the rate of technological progress that were stimulated by human capital accumulation induced a reduction in fertility rates, generating a demographic transition in which the rate of population growth declined along with an increase in the average level of education. Thus, consistent with historical evidence, the theory suggests that prior to the demographic transition, population growth increased along with investment in human capital, whereas the demographic transition brought about a decline in population growth along with a further increase in human capital formation.

Galor and Weil's theory suggests that a universal rise in the demand for human capital in the second phase of the Industrial Revolution and the simultaneous increase in educational attainment across Western European countries generated the observed simultaneous onset of the demographic transition across Western European countries that differed significantly in their levels of income per capita. In particular, the demographic transition in England was associated with a significant increase in the investment in child quality as reflected by years of schooling.

One can argue that the lack of clear evidence about the increase in the return to human capital over this period is an indication for the absence of a significant increase in the demand for human capital.

This partial equilibrium argument, however, is flawed. The return to human capital is an equilibrium price that is affected both by the demand and the supply of human capital. Technological progress in the second phase of the Industrial Revolution brought about an increase in the demand for human capital, and indeed, in the absence of a supply response, one would have expected an increase in the return to human capital. However, the significant increase in schooling that took place in the 19th century, and in particular the introduction of public education that lowered the cost of education, generated a significant increase in the supply of educated workers. Some of this supply response was a direct reaction of the increase in the demand for human capital, and thus may only operate to partially offset the increase in the return to human capital. However, the removal of the adverse effect of credit constraints on the acquisition of human capital as reflected by the introduction of public education, generated an additional force that increased the supply of educated labour and operated towards a reduction in the return to human capital.

7.3.3.2. Reinforcing mechanisms

Decline in Child Labour. The effect of the rise in the demand for human capital on the reduction in the desirable number of surviving offspring was magnified via its adverse effect on child labour. It gradually increased the wage differential between parental labour and child labour inducing parents to reduce the number of their children and to further invest in their quality. Moreover, the rise in the importance of human capital in the production process induced industrialists to support education reforms and thus laws that abolish child labour, triggering a reduction in child labour and thus in fertility.

Rise in Life Expectancy. The impact of the increase in the demand for human capital on the decline in the desirable number of surviving offspring may have been reinforced by the rise in life expectancy. The decline in mortality rates in developed countries since the 18th century and the recent decline in mortality rates in less developed countries corresponded to a gradual increase in life expectancy.

Despite the gradual rise in life expectancy prior to the demographic transition, investment in human capital was rather insignificant as long as a technological demand for human capital had not emerged. Similarly, the rise in life expectancy in less developed regions in the first half of the 20th century has not generated a significant increase in education and a demographic transition. The technologically based rise in the demand for human capital during the second phase of the Industrial Revolution and the rise in the expected length of productive life has increased the potential rate of return to investments in children's human capital, and thus reinforced and complemented the inducement for investment in education and the associated reduction in fertility rates.

Preference for Offspring's Quality: The impact of the increase in the demand for human capital on the decline in the desirable number of surviving offspring may have been magnified by cultural or genetic evolution in the attitude of individuals toward child quality. During the epoch of Malthusian stagnation that characterised most of human existence, individuals with a higher valuation for offspring quality (in the context of the quantity-quality, survival strategies) gained an evolutionary advantage and their representation in the population gradually increased. The agricultural revolution facilitated the division of labour and fostered trade relationships across individuals and communities, enhancing the complexity of human interaction and raising the return to human capital. Moreover, the evolution of the human brain in the transition to Homo sapiens and the complementarity between brain capacity and the reward for human capital has increased the evolutionary optimal investment in the quality of offspring. The distribution of valuation for quality lagged behind the evolutionary optimal level and individuals with traits of higher valuation for their offspring's quality generated higher income and, in the Malthusian epoch when income was positively associated with aggregate resources allocated to child rearing, a larger number of offspring. Thus, the trait of higher valuation for quality gained the evolutionary advantage, and the Malthusian pressure gradually increased the representation of individuals whose preferences were biased towards child quality.

This mechanism is consistent with the observed gradual rise in literacy rates prior to the Industrial Revolution. It suggests that the increase in the investment in human capital prior to the Industrial Revolution was a reflection of changes in the composition of preference for quality in the population that stimulated investment in human capital, prior to the increase in the demand for human capital in the second phase of the Industrial Revolution.

This evolutionary process was reinforced by its interaction with economic forces. As the fraction of individuals with high valuation for quality increased, technological progress intensified, raising the rate of return to human capital. The increase in the rate of return to human capital along with the increase in the bias towards quality in the population reinforced the substitution towards child quality, setting the stage for a more rapid decline in fertility along with a significant increase in investment in human capital.

7.3.4. Decline in Gender Gap

The decline in gender gap in the last two centuries is an alternative mechanism that could have triggered a demographic transition and human capital formation. The rise in women's relative wages and women's relative education in the last two centuries and its potential impact on the rise in female labour force participation and the associated decline in fertility rates have been the center of another theory of the demographic transition.

Technological progress and capital accumulation complemented mental-intensive tasks and substituted for physical intensive tasks in the industrial production process. In light of the comparative physiological advantage of men in physical-intensive tasks and women in mental-intensive tasks, the demand for women's labour input gradually increased in the industrial sector, decreasing monotonically the wage deferential between men and women. In early stages of industrialisation, wages of men and women increased, but the rise in female's relative wages was insufficient to induce a significant increase in women's labour force participation. Fertility, therefore increased due to the income e.ect that was generated by the rise in men's absolute wages. Ultimately, however, the rise in women's relative wages was sufficient to induce a significant increase in labour force participation. It increased the cost of child rearing proportionally more than households income, generating a decline in fertility and a shift from stagnation to growth.

7.3.5. Other Theories

Old-Age Security Hypothesis: The old-age security hypothesis has been proposed as an additional mechanism for the onset of the demographic transition. It suggests that in the absence of capital markets that permit intertemporal lending and borrowing, children are assets that permit parents to smooth consumption over their lifetime. The process of development and the establishment of capital markets reduce this motivation for rearing children, contributing to the demographic transition.

Although old-age support is a plausible element that may affect the level of fertility, it appears as a minor force. The importance of the decline in the role of children as assets in the onset of the demographic transition is questionable. The rise in fertility rates prior to the demographic transition, in a period of improvements in the credit markets, raises doubts about the significance of the mechanism. Furthermore, cross-section evidence in the pre-demographic transition era indicates that wealthier individuals, that presumably had a better access to credit markets, had a larger number of surviving offspring.

Exogenous Shocks - Luck: Becker, Murphy and Tamura advance a theory that emphasises the role of a major exogenous shock in triggering the demographic transition, underlying the role of luck in the determination of the relative timing of the demographic transition across nations and the wealth of nations. They argue that a major shock shifted economies from the low-output high-fertility steady-state equilibrium towards the high-output low-fertility steady-state equilibrium, triggering a demographic transition. This theory suffers from critical deficiencies in the micro-structure. Moreover, it generates predictions that are inconsistent with the evidence. In particular, in contrast to existing evidence that shows that the process of industrialisation and the associated increase in income per capita was accompanied by sharp increase in population growth, prior to their decline in the course of the demographic transition, a major shock that would shift the economy from the basin of attraction of a highfertility to a low-fertility steady-state equilibrium would generate, counterfactually, a monotonic decline in fertility rates along with a simultaneous rise in income per capita.

7.4. International Migration in Arab Countries

One of the major challenges Arab countries are faced with is international migration. This issue derives its significance from the fact that a large number of working-age people are leaving their country of origin for other countries that may offer more attractive employment opportunities and higher incomes, as well as better health and education services for themselves and their families. With the resulting demographic transition as it occurs, it is expected that the migration of the working-age population will increase, leading to an accelerated rate of international migration on the whole. It is also true, however, that as the demographic transition proceeds, a window of opportunity will began to take shape, in which the dependency ratio will decline, making savings and investments more feasible.

In evaluating the future on the basis of the current erroneous economic policies in the Arab region, there is little likelihood of benefiting from the declining dependency and taking advantage of the consequent increase in resources for investment unless effective policies are undertaken to make employment rates grow faster than the working-age population. Whether the Arab countries will be able to make the most of the emerging demographic bonus and achieve higher economic growth, thus containing international migration, will depend on how efficient their socio-economic policies are in converting the increased savings into productive investment geared to generating economic growth.

One of the predictable problems Arab governments will have to face in the near future will be the political and social pressures resulting from the growing demand by people to migrate. The policies and legislation of many countries no longer encourage migration, and the majority of receiving countries are currently seeking to limit the influx of migrants by imposing tighter control through rigid immigration policies. This paper, therefore, is formulated in accordance with the Secretary-General's recommendation that international migration should be considered a priority area of concern for the international community; and, in line with the recommendations of international conferences, the Economic and Social Commission for Western Asia (ESCWA) has given special importance to the issue of international migration in its work programme, in which the Commission calls for integrating population issues in the socio-economic planning process, thus advocating the strategy of "making the option to remain in one's country a viable one for all people."

7.4.1. Historical Perspective of Migration

Migrants can be classified in two groups, according to migration types: (1) voluntary migration, resulting from the deterioration of economic conditions in a wide range of Arab communities; this type of migration is based a voluntary personal decision; and (2) forced migration, resulting from disturbing political situations and severe local and regional conflicts; this type of migration, forced and compulsory, displaces people involuntarily.

Population mobility within the Arab region is not a new phenomenon. At the onset of the last century, movement between regions was a very easy process and did not entail any political or legislative restrictions. Following the independence of countries, however, social and economic laws were enacted to organise the population movement between countries. During the last quarter of the twentieth century, international migration within the Arab region occurred mostly in response to the economic development of the oil-rich Gulf countries, where rising oil prices considerably increased the growth rate of the gross domestic product (GDP), as well as the investment rates. To benefit from the economic wealth generated by the soaring oil prices, which ameliorated their economic and social infrastructure, the Gulf countries sought to attract workers from highly-populated countries and chose to assign high priority to the Arab labour force. This created a kind of balanced regional labour market during that period. Owing to the high oil prices, these countries managed to increase their capital accumulation and thus their economic growth, which opened up a large number of employment opportunities.

The oil-producing countries of the Gulf region thus became the main destination for migrant workers from Arab countries. At the same time, the countries from which they originated adopted a one-sided strategy, in which they viewed their industrial sector as strategic in retaining their citizens at home, by attempting to create new job opportunities and increase productivity. Coinciding with this strategy, however, were the conflicting realities of high population growth, an unfavourable age structure of the population, and a high dependency ratio. These countries were unable to absorb the vast growth in the working-age population, however, the reason being that the accumulation of GDP in the industrial sector now depended on high technology, which required technical skills that their educational and training system had failed to provide. Yet, it should be mentioned that in the last decade of the past century, international migration was also linked to other significant factors, such as political instabilities and wars, which seriously hampered socio-economic development in the region and left many people either unemployed or displaced.

At the same time, another type of migration had emerged, in which a large flow of people migrated outside the Arab region. The unfavourable demographic trend in Western countries, where fertility rates were below replacement level, had made it difficult for them to meet their labour market requirements. In contrast, population and high fertility trends in the Arab countries were moving in an opposite direction that eventually created widespread unemployment. These conditions caused a good number of Arabs to emigrate from their country in search of jobs at higher wages and a better quality of life.

7.4.2. Phases of International Migration

7.4.2.1. Phase One: balanced Arab labour market

During this phase, the process of international migration in the Arab region was interpreted in terms of labour market demand and supply. In general, that stage reflected the former role of the Arab labour market in achieving a balance between the flow of labour from countries that were highly populated but scarcely endowed to other countries that were highly endowed with oil and scarcely populated. Thus, economic prosperity as a pull factor in countries of destination has played a considerable role in decreasing unemployment in countries of origin. When the international oil prices were rectified, the Gulf countries felt compelled to adopt ambitious programmes and plans; but because of population growth, the labour force participation rate and the skills level, they were unable to ameliorate the requirements for investments.

Meanwhile, the non-oil Arab countries were experiencing a high population growth and had an overflow in their labour force, which made it normal that this surplus be used to meet the labour shortages in Gulf countries. Consequently, the Gulf countries witnessed an intensive movement of Arab labour that reached 3.14 million in emigration during the oil boom period of 1973 to 1982.

7.4.2.2. Phase Two: regressed economic growth

Because of the decline in Arab oil revenues, which had fallen to US dollar 92 billion by 1985, the oil-producing countries were forced to reconsider their economic policies and investment plans, as well as their public expenditure programmes, and allowed for only a limited number of highly skilled Arabs to enter the labour markets. The new era of restrictive measures reduced the number of projects and thus the number of employment opportunities. In many cases, the Gulf countries imposed taxes on immigrants and also refrained from the services of a great number of the existing labour force.

7.4.2.3. Phase Three: return migration

The end of the last phase marked the beginning of a new phase known as "return migration". If the economic recession during the 1980s constituted a reason for the returned labour force, the wrapping up of many infrastructure projects in a number of the Gulf countries constituted an added reason for them to return home. However, their return was gradual, which enabled the economies of their countries to accommodate them. The outbreak of the Gulf war in August 1990, however, dealt a severe blow to the economies of labour-exporting countries. The immediate implications of the conflict prompted a large and sudden Arab exodus from the Gulf countries, namely from Kuwait and Saudi Arabia, to their countries of origin, and the subsequent economic slowdown experienced by those countries led to scaling back the number of Arab migrant workers. It is important to note that despite the remittances sent by the migrants to their country of origin, those remittances did not improve productivity nor did they create new job opportunities. The unemployment rate soared and the problem of absorbing the sudden flood of returnees in the economy of the sending countries was left unsolvable for a long time. The sudden, large number of returnees put tremendous pressure on productive capacity and raised many questions on the effectiveness of remittances.

7.4.3. International Migration in the Framework of ICPD

According to the Programme of Action of the 1994 International Conference on Population and Development (ICPD), economic, political, and cultural interrelations play an important role in the flow of people between countries, whether they are developing or developed countries. International migration in its diverse types is linked to those interrelations and both affects and is affected by the development process. International economic imbalances, abject poverty, and environmental degradation, combined with the absence of peace and security, the violation of human rights, and the varying degrees of development of judicial and democratic institutions, are all factors affecting international migration. Explicably, international migration can have a positive impact on both the countries of origin and the countries of destination, providing the former with remittances and the latter with needed human resources. International migration also has the potential of facilitating the transfer of skills and contributing to cultural enrichment. However, international migration entails the loss of human resources for many countries of origin and may give rise to political, economic, or social tensions in the countries of destination.

To be of use, international migration policies need to take into account the economic constraints of the receiving countries, as well as the impact of migration on the host society as well as on the countries of origin. The long-term manageability of international migration hinges on making the option to remain in one's country a viable one for all people. Therefore, efforts to achieve sustainable economic and social development and ensure a better economic balance between developed and developing countries should be strengthened. It is also necessary to increase efforts to defuse international and internal conflicts before they escalate, to ensure that the rights of indigenous people and of persons belonging to ethnic, religious, or linguistic minorities are respected, and to respect the rule of law, promote good governance, strengthen democracy, and ensure human rights.

The ICPD Programme of Action emphasised the task of eliminating the causes of international migration, namely those related to the problem of poverty, by achieving sustainable economic growth and equitably improving the quality of life for all people. In the Millennium Declaration, strategies aimed at realising a sustainable economic growth that may alleviate poverty and foster equality between men and women are considered, along with empowering women and providing suitable and productive job opportunities for youth. In order to realise those goals, good governance should prevail in every country; enabling all citizens to participate in ensuring accountability, transparency, and the rule of law.

7.5. International Migration and Development Policies

In most of the Arab countries, past policies have ignored the human dimensions of economic development. The strategic aim of increasing economic growth through industrialisation and/or exports contributed to focusing on maximising economic growth rather than on improving the standard of living for the people. In spite of their attempts to initiate structural reforms, many countries in the region are still on a slow growth path, effectively sidelined from globalisation and the benefits of closer economic integration with the rest of the world. The countries of the region receive only one third the foreign direct investment (FDI) expected for developing countries of equivalent size, while portfolio investment is virtually non-existent, because equity markets are underdeveloped. Global financial integration lags behind that for other developing countries-less than half the Arab countries have meaningful access to financial markets. Trade performance is also below that of other regions, although oil exports continue to be a substantial source of foreign exchange earnings, despite their overall decline since 1985. As a result, the region's share of the world export market fell by more than half between 1980 and 2000, whereas the trade share of other developing regions rose slightly during that same period. It should also be noted that the region's information and technology links are among the weakest in the world-the number of Internet users per capita, for example, is quite low compared with other regions.

With the persisting slow growth of the past few decades, unemployment increased in almost all Arab countries. Consistent and comparable data on employment trends are hard to find; estimates of joblessness vary widely and come from a range of different sources.

In the Gulf countries, segmented labour markets with differential wages for nationals and non-nationals contributed to the high unemployment rate. In the private sector, employers preferred to hire expatriate labour (mostly male), since nationals were generally unwilling to work at the same wage levels as non-nationals. On the other hand, the public sector has been responsible for the absorption of nationals, particularly in the employment of women.

Furthermore, government policies that neglected agricultural development in favour of capital intensive industrialisation have created legacies of instability and promoted large-scale urban migration. The growth in the number of jobs envisioned by the industrial sector, however, was not adequate; it absorbed only a small percentage of the labour force, and an imbalance between the supply and demand of labour resulted. In addition, inequalities between the developed and the underdeveloped world, as well as real wage differentials, pushed workers to seek higher wages outside their country.

Associated with those policies, unfavourable vocational and educational policies led to a mismatch between the requirements of the labour market and the available skill level of the labour force. The main focus of the education policies adopted by Arab countries was on expanding the number of people with educational degrees rather than on providing them with the skills needed by the labour market. The educational process, by and large, was separated from the overall development process-its aim was to satisfy social preferences rather than fill the demands of the labour market. In consequence, the gap between the qualifications provided by education and the occupational skills required by the labour market was amplified. These non-integrated policies aggravated the unemployment problem, pushed the wage level further down, and caused a great number of working-age educated people to migrate to countries with higher productivity and ample job opportunities. Recently, many countries realised that out migration not only had deprived them of their best human resources, but had negatively influenced the educational system and created a situation of concern about investment in education. At the same time, policies that encouraged rural-urban migration also contributed to reducing the meagre availability of job opportunities in the manufacturing and other services sectors.

The main reasons for the recent policy changes in international migration in the region have been wars and political instability. In the aftermath of the 1990 Gulf war, the old mechanism that produced and structured the Middle East migration system ended. Policies which had previously been based on the conventional neo-classical thinking that treats migrant labour as a form of human capital and explains international mobility of labour in terms of market supply and demand were found to be no longer successful in interpreting the organisational shift that had occurred in the labour migration process. Owing to the Gulf war, the structure and character of the international migration system in the labour-receiving countries of the Gulf region collapsed and left in its wake policies based on security concerns. The old migration regime, under which Arab emigrants had enjoyed advantage as the favoured category of employees in the oil-rich countries, came to an end. Other than the war, political instability in many countries significantly contributed to international migration, forcing people to migrate to countries outside the region in pursuit of security and political stability.

Determining the current and future phase of migration calls for analysing a series of interconnected political, economic, social, and demographic factors. In view of the demographic changes, on one hand, and the evolving economic, social, and political challenges facing the region, on the other hand, initiating swift appropriate policy responses should be considered within an integrated approach that will achieve "making the option to remain in one's country a viable one for all people." One of the predictable issues Arab governments will have to face is related to the political and social pressures resulting from the growing demand for migration. The receiving countries, however, no longer encourage migration and are currently seeking to curtail its movement through the tighter control of rigid immigration policies.

On the other hand, despite the hidden momentum of population growth, the age structure of the population in the region is changing. Currently, the Arab population is youthful, making the youth dependency ratio very high, which means that the working force must support almost twice as many children as it does in low-fertility countries. Nevertheless, with the continuing trend in decelerated fertility, an opportunity to compensate for the performance of the recent past could soon emerge. As mentioned before, when fertility begins to decline, a demographic "window of opportunity" opens up, by which sustained economic growth can be generated through the increased personal savings and investment that become possible.

Judging the future on the basis of the current socio-economic situation in the Arab region, it appears clear that unless reinforcing and effective policies are taken to achieve sustained economic growth and find a niche in the global market, the consequences of unsuccessful policies and bad governance will cause the opportunity of benefiting from the demographic bonus to be missed. Such an unfortunate eventuality would reinforce the decision of people to migrate, perhaps to unfavourable regional and world political environments, in which many young men and women may find themselves prone to criminal behaviour or to engaging in political conflicts out of frustration with the hopelessness of their lives.

7.6. Conclusion

The demographic transitions that swept the world in the course of the last century has been identified as one of the prime forces in the transition from stagnation to growth. It brought about significant reduction in fertility rates and population growth in various regions of the world, enabling economies to convert a larger share of the fruits of factor accumulation and technological progress into growth of income per capita. Various mechanisms have been proposed as possible triggers for the demographic transition, and thus as a catalyst in the transition from stagnation to growth. Empirical evidence, however, suggests that the increasing role of human capital in the production process in the second phase of the Industrial Revolution was the central force behind the demographic transition. Unlike episodes of technological progress in the pre-Industrial Revolution era that failed to generate sustained economic growth, the onset of the demographic transition liberated the gains in productivity from the counter balancing effects of population growth paving the way for human capital formation and the emergence of the modern state of sustained economic growth.

References

Caldwell, John C., "Toward a Restatement of Demographic Transition Theory", *Population and Development Review* 2: 321-66, 1976.

Kuzynski, Robert R., *The Measurement of Population Growth*, Gordon and Breach Science Publishers, New York, 1969.

Shakoori Batool, "Demographic transition and its Implicaitons on Demgraphic Tranisition and its Implications on Employment and International Migration", *Fourth Coordination Meeting on Internatinal Migration,* Population Division Department of Economic and Social Affairs United Nations Secretariat, New York, 26-27 October 2005.

CHAPTER 8

Impact of Population Growth in Economic Development

8.1. Introduction

Overpopulation is a growing problem throughout the world at this stage in time. Currently, the world population has crossed over the six billion mark and is on an exponential path upwards. Economists are torn between two theories; one that states population increase and growth help a nation's economy by stimulating economic growth and development and another that bases its theory on Robert Malthus' findings. Malthus states that population increase is detrimental to a nation's economy due to a variety of problems caused by the growth. For example, overpopulation and population growth places a tremendous amount of pressure on natural resources, which result in a chain reaction of problems as the nation grows. On the macroeconomic level, it is more believable to argue that population does undermine a nation's economy because an increase in the number of people leads to an increase of the number of mouths to feed.

The increase in demand for food leads to a decrease in natural resources, which are needed for a nation to survive. Other negative effects of population growth and, specifically, overpopulation include poverty caused by low income per capita, famine, and disease. India is a prime example of Thomas Malthus' theory of population growth and its effect on the economy. India is a country plagued by poverty primarily caused by overpopulation. Inhabited by over nine hundred billion people, India has a population of three hundred million under the poverty line. A majority of the poor population is unemployed, starving, and is being forced to beg on the streets to make ends meet. Yet, the government isn't showing any apparent signs of reform to decrease poverty among their citizens, through welfare progrmmes or fiscal spending. In theory, more people may mean a country can produce and consume more goods and services, leading to economic growth. But this can only occur when employment opportunities grow at least as fast as the labor force and when people have access to the necessary education and training. This is a race that the Indian government is losing. Rapid population growth complicates the task of providing and maintaining the infrastructure, education and health care needed by modern economies.

Economists advocating the positive side to population growth, say that the growth creates new problems that in the short run constitute to a number of problems, including famine, poverty and even unemployment. Yet, they also state that in the long run, it leads to new developments, through advancement in technology, that leave countries better off than if the problems never occurred. On one hand, theoretical elements suggest that more population retard the growth output per worker. The overwhelming element in the theory is Malthusian diminishing returns to labour, as the stock of capital does not increase in the same proportion as does labour.

On the positive side, one can see a chain reaction of events caused by population growth. According to the neo-classical growth model, population is beneficial to an economy due to the fact that population growth is correlated to technological advancement. Rising population promotes the need for some sort of technological change in order to meet the rising demands for certain goods and services. With the increased populace, economies are blessed with a large labour force, making it cheaper as well, due to its immense availability. An increase in labour availability and a low cost for labour results in a huge rise in employment as businesses are more inclined to the cheap labor. Low labour costs results in a shift of money usage from wages into advancement through technology. According to this model, the technological advancement that accompanies the growth of population and the expansion of population, allows for even more population to survive due to the rise in overall outputs by the business and the nation as a whole. Thus, it generates demands for goods and results in overall economic growth. The rising population provides a supply of labor and contributes to the increase in output of goods.

8.2. Process of Economic Growth and Development

According to Julian Simon, a prestigious economist at the University of Maryland, the long run benefits of population growth that links to economic development of poor countries are on the positive balance, contrary to conventional wisdom. He figured that an increase in the numbers of consumers and an increase of income, expand the demand for raw materials as well as finished products. Naturally this would lead to a shortage in goods and services caused by the high demand for products and services, forcing up prices for the natural resources. The increased prices will trigger a search for new ways to satisfy the increasing demands in order to meet expectations. Sooner or later new sources and innovative substitutes will be found. The new discoveries lead to cheaper natural resources than existed before the increase in population and the demand for goods and services begin. In turn, it leaves a nation better off than if the shortages had never appeared, meaning the nation has gone through a process of economic growth and development.

Normally, through conventional wisdom, economists might argue that population growth and overpopulation hinders the growth output per worker. The important factor to this theory is Malthusian diminishing returns to labour, as the stock of capital, including land, does not increase in the same proportion as does labour. Another important factor, that contradicts Simon's theory, is the dependency effect, which suggests that saving is more difficult for households when there are more children and that higher fertility causes social investment funds to be diverted away from high-productivity uses. These factors seem to suggest that high fertility, and, more importantly, increasing population growth create a negative effect on output per worker, and on the broader aspect, it creates negative economic growth.

Yet, empirical data does not support this a priori reasoning. Contemporary evidence provided by a number of economists indicates there is a correlation between population growth and economic growth and development. Although most of these economists found inconsistent evidence to prove this theory, they did, generally, obtain the same data. Their reports concluded that population growth does have a positive effect on less-developed countries (LDC's).

Although some said the positive effects were very minimal and weak, the economists were still able to use a simulation model for LDC's and report that economic growth did occur.

Economists, Easterlin, Kuznets, Conlisk and Huddle, and Thirlwall all arrayed LDC's by their recent population growth rates and their economic growth rates, to examine for relationships between the two. Kuznets compiled data on 21 countries in Asia and Africa, including India. In the samples he took, Kuznets reported no significant negative correlation between population growth and the growth per capita. Conlisk and Huddle regressed the output growth rate on the savings rate and the rate of population growth of 25 LDC's, and announced that an increment of population has, ceteris paribus, a positive effect on per capita income. These empirical studies do not necessarily show that fast population growth in less-developed countries increases capita per income, although most findings reported positive effects. But they do imply that one should not assert that population growth decreases per capita economic growth in less-developed countries.

To prove this theory, put forth by population economists, a model is constructed that includes elements of the standard LDC models but it also embodies other elements: demand effects on investment, work vs. leisure choice, and variations in work activity as a function of differences in needs and standards of living and economics of scale. It also embodies shifts in labour, depreciation, and land building. The model solves the theory by utility maximisation, or finding the highest leisure-output indifference curve that touches the production function ($Q = \{L, T, K\}$).

Other economists seem to think otherwise, and oppose the theory that population growth has a positive effect on economic growth. Basic theory surrounding population growth in lessdeveloped countries states that the growth of a populace may eventually lead to overpopulation, due to the simple factors of food, education, health, housing, and employment. Earth and its resources are finite. Human ingenuity and efforts have limits to fulfill the needs of the increasing numbers. The more heads there are in a nation means there are more mouths to feed. This begins Malthus' theory of diminishing returns when it comes to resources and food. Malthus states: either people practice continence, restrain sexual impulses, or they breed themselves into starvation. Population is said to be negative once productivity and output are less than demand. Population growth, no matter how high or low it may be, results in a rise in a nation's populace. The rise in population will increase the demand for goods and services, such as food, water, and a variety of other resources needed for survival. The demand indifference curve shows us a primary problem with population growth. If supply (based on quantity and price) ends up lower than the demand for the supply of the good, the resulting effect would be that of a shortage of goods. In the long run, the resulting shortage of goods and services available to the rising population leads to starvation. Yet, starvation isn't achieved solely because of the shortage in goods. Since demands are high for resources and the resources are depleted due to the population increase, the prices of the goods are raised, causing a shift to the left in the supply curve. The rising price, in return, reduces the demand for certain goods, unless the good is a necessity for survival, causing a shift in the demand curve to the left. The decrease in demand is due to the insufficient income per capita, meaning consumers cannot afford to purchase many necessary goods in the market. Due to the fact that the goods are now unaffordable the consumers won't be able to purchase the necessary food required to survive, resulting in starvation, famine and even disease.

Another problem associated with population growth, which might lead to a decrease in economic growth, is the problem of environmental degradation and resource scarcity. Earth is comprised of 75% water, the rest is comprised of land, with a majority of it used for agriculture. According to Malthus, population growth of a nation is detrimental to economic growth, primarily due to the factor of finite resources in an economy. With a rise in the number of people, a nation can expect a decline in the natural resources and in the end a lowering of the production of goods. In a closed and stagnant economy with fixed natural resources, no capital accumulation and no technological change, population growth and size determines the standard of living as well as the state of natural resources.To some economists, rapid population growth can be associated with downward pressure on wages and worsening distribution of income, if not actual negative effects on the income per capita. This is mainly due to the spreading of capital over larger number of workers or due to the difficulties in raising the quantity and quality of investments in education and health. If it is true that continuous rapid population growth is detrimental to the growth of per capita incomes, while past population growth is beneficial to the economy once fertility decline sets in, then the ultimate impact of population growth on the environment depends on the impact made by economic growth. Past population growth seemed to be at a slower rate than what it is now, and because of that factor economic growth thrived in the past, where as now, it seems that the rapid population growth is detrimental to an economy due to its strains on resources, cause for famine, disease, poverty and even unemployment. This is why most Malthusian economists urge governments to step up and curb the rapid population growth in order to sustain economic growth.

In the case of India, one of the world's most prosperous developing nations, one can try to place India in the positive economic growth theory, or the negative economic growth theory (Malthus' theory).

India is considered a developing country, although it is one of the most affluent developing countries in the world due to recent economic growth. Government reforms over the past six years brought about an unprecedented strong economic performance. Yet at a time of economic growth, India seems to be going through an enormous population growth. Currently India has a population of over 900 million and just about to reach the 1 billion mark. Although it may seem that India is overpopulated, statistics show that the population growth rates have fallen over the years and reduced the rate of growth.

Still, overpopulation is a problem in India and has been addressed by many organisations: UNFPA, and the Population Summit, and more. According United Nations, India's population has gone from 348 million in 1950 to 850 million in 1990 to 950 million in 1998.

According to this data India's population is increasing at an average rate of 2% a year, and is gradually slowing down. The problems addressed by the United Nations, that accompany high populations, are poverty and famine. In a population of 900 million almost 300 million are under the poverty line, plagued by malnutrition, illiteracy, and social inequalities.

India seems to still sustain economic growth and stability, through growth in a variety of sectors, agriculture, industrial and the financial structure growth despite the rise in population. This is due to the low unemployment rates that attach itself to India's economy.

India has an increasing rate of employment that averages about 1.2% annually. Like its Asian neighbors, India has a large skilled work force, which, unlike other Asian nations, is protected by politically powerful unions. India also has an abundance of white-collar workers to further advance the industrial and agricultural sector, which 70% of the population depend on, is rapidly growing. Some economists say that because of India's abundance of natural resources, it could feed the whole world for the next 100 years with the increasing rate of population growth.

Industry has also grown enormously thanks to a large, skilled work force, even though salaries remain relatively low. In Bangalore, the high-technology capital, a computer programmer, with skills matching those of his peer in the United States, receives one-third the salary. Paradoxically, the government has heavily subsidised higher education while neglecting primary education. This accounts for the proportionally large number of professionals like doctors, lawyers and engineers.

India's economy, no doubt, is achieving positive balance of results from their population growth. Although one cannot say that India's population has a 100% positive effect on economic growth, but one may say that India is certainly profiting from an enormous population.

Following the neo-classical growth model, India has advanced as a result of population growth. India's GDP has increased at a steady rate and is ranked among the top among developing countries for their high rates of GDP and their steady increase of output and wealth. Yet, looking at India's GDP versus its population, in no way explains why population growth has a positive effect on India's striving economy.

A variety of factors play into the models that depict India's growing economy. Due to the rising population a large labor force is thus created. Yet the labor force never arrived from thin air. Through Indian fiscal policies, India was able to spend money on education to instruct the youth and adults, in order to help them play a productive role in India's economy. Due to the rise in the education among citizen's, India was able to generate a high employment field. The high rates of employment meant that India's economic sectors, mainly agriculture and industry, began increasing their productivity. Increase in productivity thus meant an increase in the output of goods and services. This meant that the nation could now meet demands of the rising population without having to raise prices, making necessities affordable to the poor.

The increased output that the Indian Economy achieved created a rise in micro and macro profits which would in turn lead to a rise in GDP. Through everything, India seemed to defy many economists theories that rising population growth, in essence, is detrimental to a nation. India, in fact, embraced the theories of Julian Simon, and used their disadvantage, or even advantage to further expand their possibilities. Yet, there still is a rising problem in India concerning poverty and malnutrition. But, through the theory that population growth has a positive effect on economic growth, India will prosper in the long run.

India, has become one of the world's fastest growing economies, primarily due to the rise in population growth creating a positive effect on its long run economic growth. India is now ranked one of the top producers in agriculture and is a top nation in terms of GDP in a developing country. In many cases, economists are correct in saying that population growth has a positive effect on economic growth of a nation.

References

Cassen, Robert and Contributors, "Population and Development", Old Debates, New Conclusions. Washington DC : Overseas Development Council. 1994

Simon, Julian, *Population and Development in Poor Countries*, Princeton: Princeton University Press. 1992

CHAPTER 9

Population Growth and Employment Opportunities

For most young people, finding productive and decent work is a coming-of-age symbol that marks the transition from childhood to adulthood. In finding employment, young people should gain independence and a freedom of choice about their lives. Unfortunately, the employment opportunities available to millions of young people are limited, making it inevitable that youth remain dependent on their families for a longer period of time. If family ties do not exist or break down, young people become increasingly exposed to the risks of leaving school prematurely and of being exploited in the labour force.

9.1. Labour Market and Future of Youths

In recent years increasing global unemployment has hit young people hard. The number of unemployed youth increased steadily between 1993 and 2003, to reach a current high (though continuing to increase) of 88 million unemployed youth. This places the youth share of the total unemployed at 47 per cent, a particularly troublesome figure given that youth make up only 25 per cent of the working-age population. The relative disadvantage of youth in the labour market is more pronounced in developing economies, where they make up a strikingly higher proportion of the labour force than in industrialised economies. Young people in developing regions are 3.8 times more likely to find themselves unemployed when compared with older workers. In industrialised economies, youth are 2.3 times more likely to be unemployed. Furthermore, youth in both the industrialised and developing regions are not only more susceptible to finding themselves among the unemployed; they are also more likely to be working long hours, on short-term and/or informal contracts, with low pay and little or no social protection. This is mainly a consequence of the difficulties associated with the initial school-to-work transition, the relative inexperience of job seekers and the frequent employment changes youth undertake in their search for decent and productive employment.

In the years to come the largest challenge in terms of youth unemployment will fall on developing regions. The question is whether there will be enough employment opportunities to accommodate the labour market entrants and whether such employment will be decent and productive. Current evidence shows that the regions with the largest shares of youth within the working-age population (aged 15 years and over)—South Asia, the Middle East and North Africa and sub-Saharan Africa—fare worst in terms of youth unemployment. The fate of the youth entering the labour force in the years to come will very much depend on the rate of economic growth as well as on an improvement in the employment content of growth.

In industrialised economies, where youth populations are expected to fall, the effects of demographic change are likely to reduce youth unemployment. But this will not happen automatically. Only if integrated policies to reduce youth unemployment are put into place will young people be able to overcome their relative disadvantages against older, more experienced workers.

The even more obvious gain in making the most of the productive potential of youth and ensuring the availability of decent employment opportunities for youth is the personal gain to the young people themselves. There is a proven link between youth unemployment and social exclusion. An inability to find employment creates a sense of vulnerability, uselessness and idleness among young people and can heighten the attraction of engaging in illegal activities. Also, cohorts that face particularly depressed labour markets when they graduate from primary or secondary education are—other things equal—subject to relatively higher rates of unemployment during their whole prime-age work career.

Finally, young people without a decent income cannot support themselves and will therefore be more likely to have to stay within the family household much longer than the family can afford. The extended financial burden on the household ruins the chance of the family as a whole to get out of poverty and sometimes hampers the chances of younger family members in gaining access to education (parents cannot afford to send them into education and forgo their limited earning potential) which then damages the future prospects of the younger siblings as well. It is not just the current family that gets stuck in the poverty trap but the next generation as well. For the poorest economies in the world, getting young people into decent employment means giving them the chance to work themselves and probably also their families out of poverty.

9.2. Demographic Trends and Growth of Youth Labour Force

Social attitudes and the spread of modern medicine caused both birth and death rates to decline in most countries during the twentieth century. However, death rates have typically declined first and birth rates only after several decades. This gap in time creates a bulge in the population of young people, which then works its way through the age-distribution. In general, a country proceeds through three stages of demographic shifts: In the first stage, the proportion of the young in the population rises. In the second stage, the proportion of young people declines, which of the elderly cohort increases modestly and, most importantly, that of adults of working age increases sharply. Finally, in the third stage, the proportion of working-age adults falls while that of old people rises.

By 2000, the industrialised economies were already nearing the third stage of the demographic transition; the youth share in the working-age population was already below one-fifth. Given the trend toward prolonging the period of education and delaying labour market entry, the shrinking of the youth labour force in this region is well confirmed and likely to continue. A 3 per cent decrease in the youth share of the working-age population is estimated for the 2003 to 2015 period. In order to predict the effects of a decline in the youth share on the youth unemployment rates, one can look at the experiences of the industrialised economies which first underwent the demographic shifts. A study of the United Kingdom, for example, found no evidence that the declining youth share led to a decline in youth unemployment rates. In fact, the youth unemployment rate deteriorated rather than improved during much of the period when the youth share of the labour force was falling.

The demographic trends in South-eastern Asia also indicate the movement toward the growing share of the older cohort, although at a slower pace than in the industrialised economies. With decreasing births per women in most countries of the Asian regions, one can expect a steady ageing of the population with a shift in population percentage shares from the younger to the older levels and a decrease in the youth share of the working-age population, which is exactly what is seen in the estimates for 2015. The children and youth cohorts are projected to decrease while the share of adults will increase. In the second stage of the transition, the youth labour force will continue to grow but at a smaller rate—one that is much lower than the expected increase in the adult labour force. Reduced labour force growth means that increasing productivity per labour unit becomes more critical. Historically, growth was also driven by the rapid rise in education standards, but given that the big gains in education have already been achieved, innovative mechanisms must be found to further enhance the productivity of the much slower growing total labour force.

9.2.1. Youth and HIV/AIDS

The devastating impact HIV/AIDS is having on many parts of the developing world is clear both in human terms (some 38 million individuals are currently HIV-positive and nearly 3 million AIDS deaths are estimated to have occurred in 2003) and also in economic and social terms, as the countries hardest hit by the disease struggle to cope with the multitude of adverse effects of the declining health status of their populations. The ILO recently reported that more than 26 million labour force participants are HIV-positive and found that "the inability of persons in the labour force who are HIV-positive to work when they become ill has consequences for every aspect of the social and economic context of countries, particularly in Africa".

Importantly, HIV/AIDS disproportionately affects the world's youth. UNAIDS estimates that HIV infections among young people account for fully half of the 11,000 new infections occurring each day. In total, an estimated 10 million young people were living with HIV/AIDS at the end of 2003, many of them young women: in sub-Saharan Africa, home to 6.2 million young persons who are HIV-positive, 75 per cent of them are young women. In addition, UNAIDS estimates that there are nearly 15 million AIDS orphans in the world today, a figure that is projected to rise. For example, it is projected that in sub-Saharan Africa, where there are now an estimated 12 million AIDS orphans, the number is expected to increase by 50 per cent—to 18 million—by 2010.

To protect the potential of youth in regions hardest hit by the HIV/AIDS crisis, policy-makers must act urgently and forcefully. They must acknowledge the adverse effects the disease is having on the ability of young people to find decent work and must promote basic education along with life-skills and traditional training. A comprehensive education programme must also educate youth about sexually transmitted diseases and how to prevent them. Policymakers must also work to foster alternative employment opportunities for young sex workers and for those young people who, because of economic necessity, are trapped in exploitative and potentially dangerous relationships, as well as in other harmful forms of work.

In sub-Saharan Africa the rising share of young people participating in labour markets goes in tandem with the stagnation in poverty reduction in the region, as poverty forces those who are able to work to take any employment opportunity that is offered to them. In all regions in the world, labour force participation rates for young people are lower than those for adults mainly because of the higher share of young people in education.

Both the smaller percentage of youth among the total working population and the overall decrease in labour force participation rates of youth indicate a decrease of the labour supply of youth. This follows, in part, from both declining fertility trends within most regions as well as increased education: more youth are attending school and are staying in school for longer periods of time. But it is likely that this trend also reflects that many young people are too discouraged even to enter the labour force, perceiving their chances of finding work as limited.

9.3. Trends in Youth Employment

The overall youth population grew by 10.5 per cent over the past ten years while youth employment grew by only 0.2 per cent. The picture was even more remarkable for some regions. In the transition economies the youth population grew by 10.1 per cent, whereas youth employment dropped by 11.7 per cent. In East Asia the youth population fell by 11.3 per cent but at the same time youth employment fell by 18 per cent. South-East Asia

witnessed growth in the total number of young people of 13.1 per cent but employment grew by only 0.3 per cent. In South Asia, the youth population grew by 21.9 per cent whereas employment only grew by 11.6 per cent. Finally in Latin America and the Caribbean there were 13.1 per cent more young people in 2003 than in 1993 but only 2.8 per cent more young people working.

Only the Middle East and North Africa and sub-Saharan Africa saw a relative balance between youth population growth and youth employment growth. At the same time the Middle East and North Africa still had by far the lowest youth employment-to-population ratio, with only every third young person working in 2003. In this region education enrollment rates are comparably low, especially for young women, and youth unemployment rates are high. The indicators together point to the enormous challenge the region faces in terms of its youth population. On the other hand, the youth employment-to-population ratios in sub-Saharan Africa are the second highest in the world, but one has to keep in mind that this does not say anything about the quality of the work that youth are engaged in. In fact, most jobs that were created in sub-Saharan Africa in the recent past were in the informal economy and were characterised by low earnings that were insufficient for young people to lift themselves out of poverty.

The difference between youth employment and youth population is also reflected in the employment-to-population ratios for youth, which give the proportion of those young people that work amongst all young people. In 2003 the youth employment-to-population ratio decreased over the previous decade in all regions except the Middle East and North Africa and sub-Saharan Africa, and even in these regions the increases were small. For the world as a whole less than half the total youth population was employed in 2003. In 1993 slightly more than one in two young people had work. This indicates that today less young people are employed compared with their total population size than ten years ago. However, it is important to keep in mind that the decreasing youth employment-to-population ratio could imply that more youth are voluntarily postponing employment perhaps to stay in school for longer. Given that youth unemployment rates globally are still so high, nevertheless, strengthens the case for an increasing scarcity of employment opportunities for the young population.

Unemployment rates are still considered as the most visible and obvious indicator of a youth employment challenge, which explains its selection as an indicator for monitoring the UN Millennium Development Goal to "develop and implement strategies for decent and productive work for youth". A person is only counted as unemployed if he or she is actually looking for work, which means he or she is neither discouraged nor voluntarily staying in education and training. A high rate of unemployment therefore indicates that there are many people actively looking for work but not finding any. The ILO is responsible for assembling, analysing and disseminating the data for the MDG target on youth employment.

Traditionally, the focus for discussion of youth employment challenges has been on unemployment. It is important to realise, however, that unemployment is only one aspect of labour force status. A young person can be inactive (outside of the labour force), unemployed, underemployed, employed full-time, part-time or even over-employed, with each status contributing equally to the development of young men and women as they begin their working life. An additional criticism of the aggregate unemployment for youth is that it mask information on the composition of the young jobless population and therefore misses out on the particularities of the education level, ethnic origin, socio-economic background, work experience, etc. of the unemployed. Moreover, the unemployment rate says nothing about the type of unemployment, which is a critical issue for policy-makers in the development of their policy responses.

In countries without effective unemployment support mechanisms, concentrating on unemployment also runs the risk of excluding from the analysis the less privileged population who simply cannot afford to be unemployed. In several developing countries, young people of higher socio-economic backgrounds are overrepresented in the unemployment numbers because it is only they who can afford to spend time looking for work, without incoming wages. The problem is not so much unemployment, therefore, in developing countries but rather the conditions of work of those who are employed. In such cases the indicators mentioned in section which relate more to conditions of work would be a much more informative gauge of the labour market situation of youth.

The advantage of using aggregate unemployment rates is their relative ease of collection and comparability for a significant number of countries, but looking at unemployment alone ignores other elements of the youth labour market that are more difficult to quantify. The ILO hopes that by adding its voice to a call for more detailed analysis of disadvantaged youth and their experience in both unemployment and employment, the awareness of the need to produce more detailed data at the country level will grow.

The ratios of the youth-to-adult unemployment rates are probably the best quantifier of the discrimination between young and older worker. The global youth unemployment rate in 2003 was 3.5 times that of the global adult unemployment rate, and has remained more than three times higher throughout the decade. The industrialised economies' ratio is 2.3 indicating that young people's chance to be unemployed is more than double that of adults. Even though youth unemployment increased dramatically in the transition economies, the ratio of the youth-to-adult unemployment rate declined over the past ten years as a result of the even sharper increase in adult unemployment. The same was true for East Asia where young people's risk of being unemployed was three times as high as that of adults.

9.4. Trends in Youth Unemployed Population

Not only do young people suffer from lower chances of finding employment but there are also significant differences in unemployment rates based on age, sex, and socio-economic background within the youth labour force.

With the growth in educational participation, especially at the highest level, there is now fierce competition among educated graduates for professional and high-level technical jobs. In many countries, qualified young people are currently being forced to accept employment below their skill level. Where the supply of qualified workers outpaces the increase in the number of professional and technical employment opportunities, high levels of underemployment—if defined as those working in lower-level jobs than those in which they might make more appropriate use of their skills are inevitable. In developing economies, underemployment among youth with undergraduate degrees has led to a rise in graduate study.

Structural youth joblessness, associated with economic and social disadvantages, is also a matter of concern. Almost every country shows different results in the unemployment figures according to ethnic origin, with the dominant group generally faring better than minority groups. There are only a few economies that produce data by both ethnic origin and age. Australia is one that reported 70 per cent of Indigenous young adults were neither in full-time education nor working in 2001, a share that was much higher than that for young people in general.28 In the United States it was estimated that around one third of black male teenage workers and one-quarter of black female teenagers remained unemployed in 1999, again rates that were much higher than the overall youth unemployment rates at the time.

Unemployment rates represent only the tip of the iceberg in terms of fully explaining the multitude of employment-related problems facing youth. Joblessness among young people is indeed a problem, but equally worrying is the fact that working conditions of employed young people are often substandard. Young workers are more likely to find themselves working long hours, on short-term and/or informal contracts, with low pay and little or no social protection. To substantiate this claim, one must turn to indicators relating to conditions of work, many of which are less readily available for a large number of countries and, if available, are not likely to be disaggregated along the age-breakdowns necessary to appraise the youth situation specifically.

9.4.1. Unemployment Duration

Usually, long-term unemployment leads to poverty and social exclusion, and this tends to further undermine future chances to find new work. Long durations of unemployment spells indicate a stagnant labour market, where chances to escape unemployment are limited. Information on incidences of long-term unemployment among young people is urgently needed so that policy-makers can target the particularly vulnerable youth experiencing longterm unemployment and help them re-enter productive society.

For adults, the incidences of long-term unemployment remained more or less stable. In truth, this indicator might be more useful in developed economies as young people in the poorest economies simply cannot afford to be unemployed for a long period and instead take any employment opportunity available.

9.4.1. Under Employment

Time-related underemployment is defined as all persons in employment whose hours of work fall below a certain cut-off point and who wish to work additional hours. A high rate among youth could imply that a large number of youth are accepting work conditions that are less than ideal, either because they view the work as temporary or because they do not have the confidence or voice to bargain for improved working conditions. Most of the 550 million working poor in developing economies are underemployed and wish to work more but do not get the chance. It is very likely that the share of working poor is even higher among youth than adults.

9.4.2. Informal Economy Employment

Estimates, based on a variety of methodologies, now exist but information relating to the involvement of young people in the informal economy has not yet been specifically compiled for a wide range of economies. So, although one may assume that young people are disproportionately represented in the informal economy, there are not yet adequate data to make a proper analysis. Where data are available and time-series comparisons can be made, an increasing trend in informal economy employment is evident. For a proper assessment of the issues relating to temporary work, one should seek to quantify first the various types of temporary employment within a country (on-call workers, temporary help agency workers, seasonal workers, fixed-term contracts, etc.); second, characteristics of temporary job holders (age, skill-level, sex, industry, duration, etc.); third, the success rate of the transition from temporary to permanent employment; and perhaps most importantly, the reasons for temporary work, i.e., whether voluntary or involuntary. Unfortunately, none of these elements will be easy to quantify in a systematic manner.

9.4.3. Employment and Occupation

This indicator is closely related to the status in employment indicator as well as to the informal economy employment indicator because of the evidence that the agricultural sector and the service sector in developing regions have a much higher likelihood of being dominated by informal employment. In addition, the agricultural sector is very often characterised by unpaid family work. Structural change has evolved over the past 50 years in tandem with the swift advance of technologies and the opening up of economies to international competition in the context of globalisation. Most employees today work in the services sector, often in occupations that were not imagined 50 years ago.

9.4.4. Discouraged Workers

Discouragement is a concept used to describe individuals who would like to work, but who are not seeking work because they feel or perceive that no suitable work is available. It is, therefore, a subjective measure, in contrast to the objectively-based measure of unemployment. Based on a cursory analysis of discouraged rates of youth and adults in OECD countries, the results were mixed as to which group is more affected. The percentage of discouraged workers within the population was higher for youth than adults in Belgium, Greece, Hungary, Norway, Sweden and the United States; the likelihood of a young person being discouraged was double that for an adult in the United States and ten times greater in Sweden. However, youth-to-adult incidences of discouragement were more or less the same in Australia, Canada, Finland, Italy and New Zealand.

Women are more likely to be discouraged than men. The OECD estimated that in 1993 women made up approximately two-thirds of the total of four million discouraged workers in OECD countries. In the poorest economies it is not very likely that people can afford to be discouraged, they simply have to work to survive. The difficulty with the informal economy is first in defining it and second in measuring participation in it. Changing employment arrangements require not only new ways of conceptualising the informal economy but also new approaches to measuring its size and contribution to the overall economy. The ILO Bureau of Statistics has taken a leading role in developing data collection methods, in standardising definitions and in providing technical assistance to national statistical offices to improve their data collection.

9.4.5. Vulnerability Rate

An interesting group to look at would be the sum of the unemployed plus those who are involuntarily outside the labour force. Set in relation to the total working-age population this number would give a good indication of the share of the population that society needs to worry about. In other words, such a measure would define persons who are "socially excluded", thus highlighting the segment of the population which most needs support either from social safety nets or families. To have this indicator—a measure of young people who are neither in education nor in employment—especially for young people would give policymakers a clearer idea of the extent of the untapped potential of young people who would be willing to work if properly assisted.

9.4.6. Wages

Because income surveys exist for many countries, wages by age could potentially be one of the easier indicators to collect. However, the interpretation of such an indicator proves to be difficult. Young people will naturally earn less as they lack the experience of older workers, but the question of how much "less" is acceptable and how much "less" reflects discrimination against young people is very hard to judge.

9.4.7. Indicators of Job Satisfaction

Finally, various indicators to judge differences between youth and adult job satisfaction would complete the picture of labour market conditions for young people. But the big question is how one quantifies job satisfaction and makes comparisons across countries.

Many young people from low-income households, whose parents held low-status, low paying employment, are often forced by the financial need of the family to enter the labour market at an early age and will typically end up in low-paid, precarious jobs with little prospect of future improvement. People living in chronic poverty will remain poor for much or all of their life and are likely to pass on their poverty to their children.

This cycle needs to be overcome and can best be surmounted by giving young people the opportunity to work themselves out of poverty. Poor young people whose incomes do not cover their living costs are not only a major challenge in developing countries but also in the developed economies. Most economies with a high share of youth unemployment report growing poverty among young people and acknowledge that this is the result of growing unemployment and also the increasing number of young people in casual and part-time employment.

It is during the formative stages of life—childhood, adolescence and youth—that long lasting aspects of personal development take place and determine "success" or "failure" later in life. With this in mind, it becomes all the more crucial that youth employment challenges are addressed and solutions developed to enhance and fulfill their potential and ensure decent employment opportunities for youth. The integration of young people into decent and more productive employment is the key challenge for national governments, the social partners, civil society, United Nations agencies and the Bretton Woods institutions.

References

Fitzenberger, B., et al., "The gender gap in labor market participation and employment: A cohort analysis for West Germany" *Journal of Population Economics,* 17, No. 1 (2004): 83-116.

McArdle, Nancy with Jan Erik Hall and Peter Zlotnick, "Population and Employment Decentralization Trends as of 1986", Joint Center for Housing Studies of Harvard University. Working Paper W88-2. Cambridge, MA. 1988.

Puhani, P.A., "Poland on the dole: The effect of reducing the unemployment benefit entitlement period during transition" *Journal of Population Economics,* Vol. 13, No. 1, 35-44, 2000.

Roed, K. and M. Nordberg, "Have the relative employment prospects for the low-skilled deteriorated after all?" *Journal of Population Economics,* 17, No. 1, 2004.

CHAPTER 10

Biological Factors of Population Growth

Evolution is a creative development from simple to complex, rather than the product of chance and selection. Evolutionary processes are generated causally but their development is open and generates diversity, novelty and complexity beyond those present in their simpler origin. The development of an organism originates with and is guided by genetic structures and creates unique and more complex organisms. In a similar manner, both physical and evolutionary processes may originate with and be guided by generic mathematical and physical relations. The formation of structures and systems is one such generic process, as demonstrated by endosymbiosis and pluricellularity. The role that such feedback processes may play in the evolution of species with mathematical models, analyses of empirical data of population numbers, and a multi-agent simulation model. Population studies provide numerical data for mathematical analysis, and we shall see the results obtained indicate creative patterns of change compatible with evolutionary processes rather than with stationary models. Although evolutionary theory and population dynamics have traditionally been separate scientific fields, evolution can be fast, as illustrated not only by the rapid mutations of viruses but also by observations with birds. Ecological and evolutionary dynamics can occur on similar timescales, so population cycles can be transformed into creative processes.

10.1. Generation of Biotic Patterns

Recursions of bipolar (positive and negative) feedback such as $A(t+1) = \sin((A(t)*t) + A(t)$ generate a pattern characterised by features of creativity called bios because It is identified in biological series. Mathematical bios is chaotic insofar as it is aperiodic, deterministic, and extremely sensitive to initial conditions. Biotic processes are radically different from chaotic attractors in being contiguous and creative. A discrete time series is contiguous when consecutive terms are similar to each other, while consecutive terms often lie on opposite sides of the median in random and chaotic series. Creativity can be operationally defined by the demonstration of three related characteristics: diversification, complexes and novelty in causal processes. Chaotic attractors do not display these properties.

Diversification, complexes and novelty can be measured with the Bios Data Analyser, which compares the series with copies randomised by shuffling. These methods are described below along with analyses of empirical series. Biotic series are clearly differentiated from similar stochastic series by analysing the time series of differences between consecutive terms, which is chaotic or biotic in the case of deterministically generated bios, and random in the case of random walks.

These time series analyses show that many processes commonly regarded as chaotic or stochastic actually are biotic. These include Schrödinger wave function and the temporal distribution of galaxies representing the expansion of the universe, suggesting that cosmological evolution may be determined by causal physical forces, rather than result from expansion of random non-homogeneities. Biotic patterns are found in heartbeat intervals, respiration, sequences of bases in DNA, the shape of rivers and shorelines, meteorological data, and economic series.

Biotic patterns as well as periods and chaos, are generated by recursions of bipolar feedback which include a conserve term + A(t); recursions without it produce only chaos. Unipolar feedback, such as the logistic equation, produces chaos, but not bios. Bipolar feedback is evident in empirical processes that generate bios. For instance heartbeat intervals are regulated by the antagonistic action of the sympathetic accelerating and parasympathetic decelerating nerves, economic prices are affected in opposite manner by supply and demand, and the Schrödinger equation involves wave functions.

10.2. Population Dynamics

Empirical data were obtained from the Global Population Dynamics Database maintained by the NERC Centre for Population Biology, Imperial College, London. All the animal populations examined show an increase in standard deviation (SD) with embedding (local diversification), as also observed with biotic series, random walks and many creative natural processes. The SD does not increase in shuffled copies of the data. Random distributions and chaotic attractors maintain a stable variance regardless of sample duration or embedding. Episodic patterns are most evident in recurrence plots. Distinct clusters of recurrences with different patterns separated by recurrence-free intervals are evident in the recurrence plots of muskrat, beaver, fox and salmon populations, as well as in biotic series and in brown noise. Shuffling erases these complexes. Lynx and vole populations show more regular clusters, reminiscent of the sequences of identical clusters of recurrences observed with periodic series. Random and chaotic series show uniform recurrence plots, without clustering.

Recurrence quantification measures innovation. Since a recurrence is a repetition of pattern, a lower than random recurrence rate indicates that the process under consideration innovates more than chance events. Novelty is thus defined as the increase in recurrence isometry produced by shuffling the data. Novelty is an essential feature of bios, which differentiates it from chaos. It initially is a surprising property, but living processes characteristically vary faster than random via specific mechanisms such as sexual reproduction, meiosis, and the induction of mutation by radiation and by stress.

The time series of the differences between consecutive terms in population time series showed complexes in all 6 species, and novelty in muskrat, beaver, salmon and red fox. Thus changes in population number are not random. This conclusion was supported by statistical analysis that showed partial autocorrelation for several lags, as observed in causal processes but not in random walks.

In summary, all six species showed deterministic causation, diversification, and contiguity, and five of them met all the criteria for bios including contiguity, aperiodic pattern, complexes, and novelty. Diversification, complexes, and novelty, exclude white noise or chaos. The observation of organisation in the time series of differences indicates causal rather than stochastic origin. The dual, accelerating and decelerating innervation of the heart, the prototype of bios, suggested to us the importance of bipolar, positive and negative, interactions; indeed, bios is generated mathematically by trigonometric functions that model bipolar feedback.

10.2.1. Population Dynamic Models

The model is stable within a relatively small range of parameters, within which all three populations show biotic time series with diversification, complexes, novelty, and deterministic causation (partial autocorrelation for several lags, pattern in the series of differences between consecutive terms). Thus using multi-agent instead of differential equations shows that food chains generate creative biotic patterns instead of periodic or chaotic ones. Previous studies have shown that indeed prey-predator relations often generate complex patterns.

10.2.1.1. Bios theory of evolution

The above studies have been guided by a new theory of evolution as a causal and creative process that applies to physical, biological and human processes. As in the parallel study of quantum processes and cosmological evolution presented at this meeting by Thomas et al, the empirical studies presented here show biotic organisation. They do thereby provide support for the notion of causal and creative development. In population data, pattern in the sequence of differences and partial autocorrelation demonstrate deterministic causation, diversification and novelty signify creation, and the succession of different complexes indicates rapid change compatible with fast evolution. Standard evolutionary theory postulates (1) biological variation resulting from accidental events (2) competition for scarce resources; and (3) selection by survival of the fittest. In contrast, the bios model of creation proposes that (1) biological diversification, novelty and complexity largely result from causal processes; (2) synergy and abundance are as important as antagonism and scarcity, and together constitute bipolar feedback processes that generate diversity, greater than random novelty, and complexity; (3) survival has priority but complex processes have supremacy in both variation and selection. Action, bipolarity and connectedness are generic features of natural processes sufficient to generate diverse, novel and complex life-like (biotic) patterns, as illustrated by mathematical recursions.

Biological actions are physical actions, i.e. changes of energy in time. Time implies unidirectionality, which is imprinted as asymmetry in biomolecules (Pasteur), embodied as sequential order in processes, and more generally manifested as causality. A physical action causes consequences; there are no isolated events. Thus evolution must be causal, not random. Processes are sequences of actions, or more properly lattices, as actions interact, converge, and bifurcate. Causal actions can generate biological variation, as illustrated by the novelty generated by biotic feedback, sexual reproduction, meiosis, the induction of mutation, and the invention and spread of new behaviours by brained organisms that establish new forms of selection. Thus sequences of actions also become imprinted as hierarchies of complexity.

Just as physical processes are ordered by fundamental symmetries described by mathematical groups, biological processes involve fundamental symmetries. Opposites not only encode information but they also generate it as diversification and novelty. Sexual procreation is exemplary. Notwithstanding, conflict over scarce resources has been regarded as the fundamental motor of change in nineteenth century theories of biological evolution and of economic processes still regarded as current.

Correspondingly, the effects of intra and interspecies competition in driving population dynamics have been emphasised. More recently, the importance of positive interactions between species as well as the coexistence of positive and negative effects have been recognised. Competition of scarce resources generates unipolar feedback, such as the logistic equation, which can generate chaos but not bios, which is the pattern actually observed in population dynamics as well as in economic processes. Bipolar opposition can generate bios. Both abundance and scarcity of the multiple biological and non-biological components of life occur in ecological communities.

Cooperation among species is as common as competition. Multicellular organisms cannot live and reproduce without the participation of intracellular mitochondria and extracellular microorganisms. Earth needs the intestinal flora, and plants require symbiotic fungi, pollinators, and other birds, mammals or insects that spread their seeds. One quarter of all documented fungi are lichenised; trees need fungi to develop; ants have cultivated fungi for over 50 million years. The importance of synergistic processes for life and its evolution is well known although surprisingly absent from neo-Darwinist discussions. Notably, competition appears to be more important where there is great abundance, such as the tropical areas studied by Darwin, while cooperation among species appears to be more obvious under harsh conditions such as the Siberian plains studied by Kropotkin, the theorist of evolution by mutuality.

Ideological differences may have been more important than climatic ones in determining the opposite sign of these two theories of evolution. Incorporating synergy and antagonism, heterotrophy is far more basic than competition in biological dynamics, and it also embodies the incorporation of simpler components to generate complex systems. System formation is exemplary of synergy.

Life evolves as a narrow layer of matter in which atoms nucleate to form systems: molecules, cells, organisms, communities. The formation of materials by other organisms allows the emergence of new and often more complex organisms, a fact that is obvious but not trivial. In genome transfers pre-formed materials drive and direct change. Genetic exchange is co-creation. Organisms can supply each other with genes and even complete genomes. Aggregation, endosymbiosis, pluricellularity, multispecies communities, and sociality are essential for evolution. The intracellular incorporation of microorganisms as mitochondria and chloroplasts are necessary for higher form of life, and in fact the very origin of eukaryotes may have been a cellular fusion between bacteria and archea. Far from leaving microorganisms behind on an evolutionary ladder, people more complex creatures are both surrounded by them and composed of them. Endosymbiosis allows pluricellularity: there are no multicellular organisms composed of prokaryotic cells. Symbiogenesis theory states that species arise from the merger of independent organisms through symbiosis.

Evolution occurs in the context of biological communities in which continual interactions exclude the occurrence of isolated events. Individuals and species do not interact at random as gas molecules but co-evolve within a web with rich topological structure. The biotic web involves hierarchical lattice structures (e.g. food chains) and processes (e.g. evolution from simple to complex organisms) and group properties at multiple levels, such as the circulation of energy and matter within and among organisms. Thus lattice, group and topological properties are intrinsic to the evolving biosphere. Connectedness provides a multidimensional form of causation capable of generating biotic patterns of population dynamics, as illustrated by simple multi-agent simulation models. It departs from simple causality that determines the outcome instead of creating complexity) as well as from stochasticity, which makes the unlikely assumption that events are independent from each other. The circulation of energy, information and matter are cyclic engines that can generate complexity, as illustrated by mathematical recursions. Species do not evolve in isolation while the biosphere remains stable as a homeostatic superorganism (Gaia). The biosphere evolves as a totality, creating multiple levels of complexity.

These multiple levels of complexity are connected in feedback processes. Thus it is proposed to split the concept of primacy into the complementary categories of priority and supremacy taking as a model the mammalian central nervous system, in which the lower and simpler bulbo-spinal levels have evolutionary and functional priority and the more recent and more complex brain cortex has functional supremacy. Simple processes and structures have priority in time and in urgency: respiration precedes and is indispensable for thinking; simple processes also are more global and hence involve greater changes in energy. Complex processes and structures emerge later in evolution but acquire local supremacy because of their greater informational content. The physical and chemical processes and products of abiotic evolution initiate and modulate biological evolution. Simple molecules constitute the biomolecules that form cells. The production of materials by simple organisms propels the creation of higher species. The complex biological processes generated by evolution alter drastically the physically composition of the planet, and thereby feedback upon biological evolution. The generation of materials such as oxygen by simpler organisms propels the creation of higher species by providing necessary materials and by generating conditions that allow for respiratory processes and are incompatible with many preexisting lifeforms. This illustrates the priority of simple organisms and the supremacy of more developed ones as a cyclic engine of evolution. Photosynthesis, sexual reproduction, and brain function redirect natural selection. Darwin highlighted the roles of sexual selection and of cooperation; he did not reduce evolution to survival, much less to struggle. The evolution of complex behaviour and brains add complex selection factors that frequently are more operative that survival.

Hierarchical relations among species are more significant than intrinsic "fitness". Cows multiply and elephant populations dwindle because of their relation to the dominant mammalian species, and AIDS viruses burgeon because they have made us their host, although through commitment to science we have become able to eradicate smallpox.

Topological connectedness is a generic property of natural processes; positing independent random events and single genes or individuals as the units of evolution represent unlikely speculations. The conservation of genes in biology (e.g. the pervasive role of hox genes) is as fundamental as the conservation of matter in physics.

10.2.1.2. Evolution is creation

Unbiased consideration of evolution from protokaryotic cells to mammals indicates an overall increase in complexity as proposed by Lamarck. Pointing to extinction and involution (e.g. parasites), Neo-Darwinian theorists assert that evolution is directionless.

Gould argues that the fact that most forms of life increase in size and complexity is an "artifact" resulting from the circumstance that life begun at the extreme of smallness and simplicity. Evolutionary progress may be explained as an obligatory sequence: creation must necessarily precede (and exceed) destruction, and simplicity must necessarily precede complexity. Constructive processes create higher levels of complexity. Complexity is the necessary result of the fact that creative processes are inherently self-conserving while destructive processes are limited to what has been constructed before. This asymmetry between construction and destruction is a necessary logical relation (tautology), which is a creative. Thus evolution has a direction towards greater complexity, including the formation of minds that create meaning, and in this sense evolution is meaningful. Evolution is creation, and creation is evolutionary, not a single event in the distant past.

Creation is necessarily accompanied by destruction: evolution includes and requires the death of individuals and the extinction of species. Involution occurs. Progress is not unavoidable. Evolution is a creative process, not a deterministic one. It is thus crucial to consider responsibly our role as dominant species. Given the human implications of evolutionary ideas, it behooves us to evaluate our assumptions in the light of all scientific disciplines, from mathematics to psychology, and to be critical of ideology. Making "selfish genes" the units of evolution is unscientific. Genes do not have self because they do not have brains and therefore cannot be selfish. What is absurd from the perspective of one science cannot be useful as a metaphor in another discipline, much less true in reality. Genes only function in context: the same set of genes is present in very different tissues, and different species share many genes, and differ only on their expression. Likewise the portrait of evolution as a chronic, bloody competition among individuals and species is at variance with growing knowledge that shows that forms multiply and grow more complex by incorporating others.

Life does not take over the planet by combat, but by networking. The notion of scarcity and struggle as the motor of change was born in political economics (Malthus) where it led to predictions that have been refuted empirically. Mathematical, physical and psychological sciences offer biology a different, richer and more solid set of assumptions. Lattice, group, and topology, the mother structures of mathematics (Bourbaki), describe generic properties of natural processes embodied at multiple levels of organisation, from quantum physics up to and including psychological structures. Evolutionary processes, as all other physical processes, are by necessity shaped by these logically necessary mathematical relations, and indeed biotic webs display lattice, group and topological properties. The asymmetry of time, informational oppositions, and tridimensional matter embody lattice order, group symmetry and topological connectedness. Recursions abstracting these features are sufficient to generate steady states, cycles, chaos and bios; these patterns are found in many processes from physics to psychobiology, and are therefore likely to be the product of causal and generic processes rather than the product of chance or of specific mechanisms.

Evolution is the necessary consequence of causal action, bipolar feedback (synergy and antagonism), and the combination and conservation of material structures in topological webs with lattice and group organisation. Just as physical processes are articulated in terms of causal equations that reflect these generic mathematical structures, the biological processes will be similarly described. Causal action, bipolar opposition (positive and negative, synergy and antagonism), connectedness, and systematic creation of complexity oppose the concepts of random change, scarcity, struggle for survival, independent events, genes or individuals, and directionless evolution advanced by standard evolutionary theory. Recognising that evolution has direction points to the existence of meaning, and its sensitivity to human intervention extends it to human beins.

References

Colin Clark, "Population Growth and Land Use", 2nd ed. *an analysis of specific problems*, 1977.

Dasmann, Raymond F., "Environmental Conservation", 5th ed., *a study of the human influence on nature and its consequences for human population*, 1984

Keyfitz Nathan (ed.), *Population and Biology: Bridge Between Disciplines*, a collection of papers on biological aspects of demography, 1984.

CHAPTER 11

Health Aspects of Population Growth

Both developed and developing countries have achieved major gains in health and survival since the beginning of the twentieth century. However, benefits have not accrued evenly across socio-economic groups. Better-educated people everywhere stay healthier and livelonger lives. The strength of education as a policy lever in social and economic development has been recognised at the national and international levels. The implications for health and mortality of the persistence and further widening of education differentials are dire, given the powerful association among education, health and mortality.

11.1. Mortality in Developed Countries

Education is a strong predictor of the health and mortality experience of individuals and their households in developed countries. Education differentials in health and mortality exist in all societies, irrespective of development policies, health-care systems or mortality levels. Education differentials in health and mortality are also not limited to particular ages, although the evidence discussed here relates to adults. Education differentials in mortality in Europe are well documented. In Russia, between 1979 and 1989, less educated groups persistently experienced higher mortality than better-educated persons. Differentials in mortality were larger for younger than for older adults. For each age group and sex, the relative advantage of better-educated persons in Russia increased between 1979 and 1989. Education differentials were also larger for men than for women.

Infectious and parasitic diseases, respiratory diseases, accidents, violence, suicide, and factors directly related to alcohol appear to have been the causes of death associated with the widest education differentials in Russia. The difference in contraceptive prevalence between those with no schooling and those with secondary education averages 29 percentage points in sub-Saharan Africa, 23 percentage points in Latin America and the Caribbean, and 19 percentage points in Asia. Even a small amount of schooling has a significant impact on contraceptive behaviour. Contraceptive-use differentials by education are most marked in sub-Saharan Africa, the region with the lowest level of education and the lowest level of contraceptive prevalence among women in the world. In this region, the percentage using contraception among married women with a secondary or higher education is more than three times as high as that among married women with no education. In the developed countries, where contraceptive prevalence is already high, differentials in contraceptive use by educational level are very small. In conclusion, evidence confirms that education has a major impact on the level of fertility, especially in developing countries.

In developed countries, education exerts a strong impact not so much on the level of fertility as on the timing of first births and the degree of childlessness. Female education was also found to be associated with fertility preferences, adolescent fertility and contraceptive use, with better-educated women desiring smaller family sizes, having lower percentages of pregnant women or mothers among their adolescent population, and having a higher percentage of women using contraception among their married population. Although the net effect of female education decreases significantly when other factors related to fertility such as household and community socio-economic characteristics (for example, income, urbanisation, aggregate levels of schooling) are controlled for, it remains a significant factor in determining fertility, and its effect on marital fertility is usually higher than the effect of husband's education or of household income.

In developing countries, education, especially that of mothers, has been found to significantly differentiate levels of child mortality. In practically all countries, children of uneducated mothers have higher relative risks of dying in early childhood than the children of mothers with primary education. Similarly, the children of mothers with primary education show higher mortality than the children of mothers with secondary or higher education. Secondary-primary differentials are generally larger than the differentials between those with no education and those with primary education.

Differentials in health-related knowledge and behaviour underlie education differentials in child mortality in developing countries. In countries such as Chad, Ethiopia, Madagascar, the Niger and Nigeria, differentials in measles immunisation across education groups are large, with barely 1 in 4 children born to uneducated mothers being immunised against measles. The children of less educated mothers are also more likely to be at a nutritional disadvantage, relative to the children of better-educated mothers.

Access to, and use of, qualified medical care at delivery are also strongly related to the level of education of the mother. Educated mothers are much more likely than uneducated ones to receive good-quality care during pregnancy and delivery, thus lowering their chances of succumbing to complications during pregnancy. The fate of mothers at delivery is particularly grave when they have no one assisting them during delivery. This predicament is most common among uneducated women. In addition to their greater likelihood of knowing about health interventions and using health services, educated women marry and enter motherhood later and have fewer children, thereby reducing their chances of maternal mortality. In contrast, the higher fertility among women of lower education status and their poor delivery care increase their risk of maternal and child ill health and mortality. Maternal death can also have deleterious consequences for the orphaned children.

An apparent difference between the United States and Europe is that in the United States, years of schooling affect equally the mortality of men and women, while in European countries, mortality for males appears to be more responsive than that for females to additional education. There are large sex differentials in life years gained from an additional year of education for Denmark, Hungary and Sweden. In all cases, except England and Wales, males gain more longevity from an additional year of education than females. At each level of education, however, the death rates for males remain well above the death rates for females. Investigations of education differentials in mortality have been less extensive in Canada.

11.2. Health Education

Health, for quite long time, could hardly find a place in our common man's need hierarchy, despite the motto, health is wealth advocated by those people who knew the benefits of it and had access to the services. Food, shelter, occupation and other socio-economic amenities remained predominantly the common man's felt-needs. Due to lack of awareness and sensitivity, his perception of health has been that a person who is visibly not sick and looks stout, is healthy as against a lean and thin looking person presumably unhealthy. In his such perception, mental and social elements rendering the man weak and unfit to do his routine chores, earn livelihood and lead a normal life, generally do not find reflection. Absence of infirmity or disease and good physical appearance seemed to dominate until recent past as the only indicators of his perception of health. He could not perceive his health as an essential element to improve his quality of life. It were the development processes initiated through government's Five Year Plans starting from early 1950's, dissemination of information and continued emphasis on literacy, health, population control measures and use of media, which sensitised a large section of people, influenced their thinking process, attitude, and enabled them to perceive and understand things in their right perspective.

As a result, now a common man's perception of health is more than merely absence of infirmity or disease, i.e. complete well being that could enable him to do his routine work, earn livelihood and lead a good life. Now, he knows considerably about his rights, demands for the same and wants to remain healthy. The swelling crowds to health quacks, private practitioners, dispensaries, hospitals, and pharmaceutical shops testify this change in common man's perception of health and the resulting health behaviour.

Health is an essential input to human resource development culminating into behavioural transformation that influences the quality of life and status of society. Health, more appropriately, public health was elaborately defined in 1920 by C.E.A. Winslow as the science and art of preventing disease, prolonging life and promoting health and efficiency through organised community efforts for sanitation of environment, the control of communicable infections, the education of individual and personal hygiene, the organisation of medical and nursing services for the early diagnosis and preventive treatment of disease, and the development of the social machinery to ensure everyone a standard of living adequate for the maintenance of health, so organising these benefits to enable citizen to realise his birthright of health - health and longevity.

11.2.1. Health Concept and Development

Historically, the concept of health with its reflection in modern system of medicine and treatment came to India with the British rule. It functioned as a close-system, limited especially to British residents in India, Government employees and military personnel. As a result, it created the impression of an alien system among the majority of people unable to identify it with their indigenous systems of medicine, which until then and later, were being resorted to by the needy. On the other hand, it was grossly inaccessible to the common masses. This situation had indicated the need for modern health care. Some efforts were made to provide health facilities, like control of epidemics, setting up of civil hospitals in some urban areas and a few rural dispensaries in outlying areas. Obviously, neither the health care planning nor medical education were based on the health needs of the people.

11.2.2. Rural Health Infrastructure

India after having signed the Alma-Ata Declaration in 1978, became committed to attaining the goal of 'Health for All' by 2000 AD through its primary health care approach. In this context, the Government revised its strategy and laid down national norms for providing and strengthening health infrastructure and aimed to make the services easily accessible to rural and tribal population all over the country and thus ensure a better population coverage. Under this approach, a 3-tier health care delivery system is made functional with 3 types of health institutions and different cadre of staff.

11.2.3. Reproductive Health

Human sexuality and reproductive health are two inseparable entities of human life. They influence each other, compliment/supplement each other, and shape the reproductive profile of both, male and female in the society.

There is a general feeling that the RH, interchangeably RCH concept is not new, as the maternal and child health, sexually transmitted disease (STD) related and all other services or programmes did exist before. But as has already been referred to above, they were available as vertical programmes, instead integrated services. Also, such programmes and services were not focussed nor the approach of service delivery was holistic. But there are health scientists, policy and programme administrators and social scientists who decipher RH as a new concept since it imbibes all these above attributes in its scope which extends even beyond these recognising reproductive rights and reproductive health as important elements of development that includes fertility regulation besides other important variables.

The RH is a new conceptual reality, i.e. a shift from the rhetoric to reality that enshrined the ICPD Cairo Programme of Action for developing countries faced with population problem on the one hand and reproductive health and gender related issues on the other. With its broad base and wide scope, the focus of RH services is confined not only to women and men but extends to the children and special population of adolescents, menopausal women and older people. The concept eludes gender (male/female) inequity and class differentiation.

Where the RH concept articulates human rights into reproductive rights, particularly reproductive rights of the woman, i.e. right to information, choice of contraception, have children, when and how many, right on her own body, and safe sex, it also stresses the constellation of women centred services, easily available and accessible to them.

The RH aims to provide need based, client centred, demand driven and high quality services to people. The Government of India's RCH programme aims to contribute to population stabilisation, sustainable development, and meeting the RH needs of women, children and adolescents within the framework of reproductive rights, gender equity and human dignity, thereby making it a composite programme.

The definition of reproductive health reflects the WHO definition of health but it encompasses much more diversified areas establishing linkages and necessity for sustainable development through humane policy and programme approach, instead of demographic targets or population stabilisation. Accordingly, the population issue could be tackled within the ambit of more comprehensive strategy of health care and socio-economic development, thereby gender equity, empowerment and status of women become crucial and male responsibility critical. This refers to desired world-wide shift in the attitude to recognise reproductive rights as human rights, women and adolescents' needs and provision of service delivery.

The encouraging advice that the implementing governments and voluntary agencies could derive from these principles is that they should not wait for more resources rather utilise the existing ones. Further, the programmes should be developed and implemented so strategically that they should meet also the needs of special circumstances and populations besides assuring and providing comprehensive and good quality care. The most significant guidance that these principles ought to provide is emphasis on the inclusion of the women's rights, empowerment in the RH programme, making them explicitly mandatory. This suggests a landmark departure from the earlier approach of health care to an integrated approach to RH, which is more pragmatic and holistic in nature.

The Government of India, Ministry of Health and Family Welfare upholds the legitimate right of its citizens to be able to experience sound RH. Accordingly, the RCH programme mission is to provide need based, client centred, high quality services to all the citizens of the country. As reflected in the preceding pages and also visualised, the RCH programme is more significant to contribute to the population stabilisation to a level that should be optimal to meet the need of national development. For this, what is contemplated important, is conformity with small family size norm. The RCH programme, thus, envisages in this direction to facilitate the availability and accessibility of the available spacing and terminal methods of family planning to the couples on the one hand and provide high quality care to the mother and child as an assurance to good health and longevity of the both on the other. The Government has taken the congnisance of the fact that for the success of the RCH programme and population stabilisation, its own efforts may not be enough, the involvement of NGOs and community is, therefore, equally important. Accordingly, the programme objectives have been laid down with such crucial concerns.

11.3. HIV/AIDS

Education - that is to say, creating awareness - is an important and essential preventative measure to slow the spread of the HIV/AIDS epidemic in all countries. In developing countries, where HIV/AIDS has taken a heavy toll in mortality and morbidity, the use of condoms as a method of prevention has been promoted actively. Yet the data show that this information has not been well assimilated and that substantial differentials exist across education groups. For example, almost all surveys indicate that uneducated women are less likely to know that condom use prevents HIV transmission.

However, even among the educated, in some countries large majorities of women do not know that condoms help protect against HIV/AIDS. Perhaps information, education and communication (IEC) messages have failed to reach their targets. Alternatively, those who receive the message may not be acting on it. This is consistent with the observation that women may view condoms mainly as contraceptives and not as a method of prophylaxis against AIDS. An important aspect of the relationship between HIV/AIDS and education is the threat that the epidemic poses to the survival of education systems in high-prevalence developing countries. The education systems of high-HIV prevalence countries are being challenged by high levels of teacher attrition and absenteeism because of HIV/AIDS-related illness and death among teachers. The epidemic inflicts heavy burdens on students and their families, often resulting in declining school enrolments and increasing dropout rates. As education systems are weakened by the HIV/AIDS epidemic, teaching and learning are becoming less effective for many segments of population. Health and mortality differentials are likely to become more pronounced because better-educated persons will protect themselves more effectively in adverse health environments. In conclusion, among the socio-economic variables that are associated with differentials in health and mortality, education has shown effects that are among the strongest and the most consistent. The reasons for the widespread education differentials in health and mortality in both developing and developed countries are not completely understood.

In developing countries, empowerment of individuals to take better control over the inherent health risks of their environment appears to play an important role. In developed countries, lifestyle factors such as smoking and excessive alcohol consumption have been implicated. It is puzzling that, with respect to HIV/AIDS, behaviour change among both the educated and uneducated groups in many countries has not, at present, been found to be very strong. Whatever the causes, the existence of large education disparities in health and mortality suggests that internationally agreed targets for the reduction of mortality and the achievement of Health for All goals are not likely to occur without major improvements in access to education, especially in developing countries. Since education is associated with lower mortality and better health in virtually all contexts, regardless of educational philosophy and orientation, expanded access to education is likely to lead to gains in health and survival. In brief, for both children and adults, better education is associated with significant improvements in health, reduction of mortality, and longer life.

11.3.1. AIDS Awareness Education

In the health sector one of the medical triumphs has been the eradication of small pox. Now one of the medical tragedies is AIDS. AIDS has become one of the dominant public health concerns today. It is caused by HIV, which is transmitted mainly through sexual intercourse. The virus can also be transmitted through contaminated blood and from mother to child. There is no cure. That the cure will be found in the immediate future is considered unlikely. Preventive education is therefore the only means of preventive HIV AIDS.

About 30.6 million people world wide were infected with HIV in 1997. More than 90 per cent of these infected persons will be in developing countries. The increase in the number of AIDS cases in Asia is showing the same trend as in Africa. Since the first reported case of AIDS in the Asian region was in the late 80s it is estimated that the graph for Asia ten years later would look exactly as the graph for Africa stands now. While there will be a decline in the number of AIDS cases in the other continents the number in Asia would only increase in the next few years.

The Statewise status of HIV/AIDS in India as reported to the National AIDS Control Organisation (NACO) shows that the figures are rising with every report that is received from each State in the country. It is also important to know that as these figures are based on the reported cases, they do not represent the actual cases. WHO/UNAIDS estimated that India had about 5 million persons with HIV in 1998.

AIDS does not discriminate between classes, castes or communities. It spreads rapidly among people with high-risk behaviours such as persons who have multiple sex partners and injecting drug users who share needles. The infection then spreads in the general population covering all segments of society. The world faces other killer diseases like malaria, tuberculosis and diarrhoea, which are preventive and curable. These diseases claim millions of lives. Among the vulnerable are mostly the young or the aged. But AIDS primary attack men and women in their economically productive years when they provide the major labour force. It, thus, threatens the development prospects of the whole nation. Women are biologically and socially more vulnerable to HIV infection than men. Male to female transmission is 2-4 times more efficient than female to male. The low status of women in society inhibits their ability to protect, it is not always possible for her either refrain from sex with her husband if she feels he is unfaithful or to convince her husband to use a condom. In addition, infected mothers can transmit HIV to their foetus and newly born babies. This can have serious impact on our efforts to reduce infant mortality in the country.

Youth in the age group 15-20 years constitute nearly one third of the population. Majority of the infected individuals belong to the age group 20-45 years, which is approximately another 30% of the population. 10 years from now, the individuals who are between the ages of 15-20 will be in the age group 15-25 and those in the age group 20-45 years will be in the age group 30-55 years. While those in the age group below 20 years have not formed their risk behaviour patterns, those in the age group above 20 years have formed their risk behaviour patterns. It is, therefore, possible to educate and prevent the youth in the age group 15-20 years to form their behaviour on the basis of information and knowledge related to HIV & AIDS transmission.

AIDS is a concern caused by a virus. AIDS arises from damage to immune system acquired as a result of infection with HIV (Human Immunodeficiency Virus). There are many conditions which can result in someone being diagnosed as having AIDS but what links them all is a deficiency or weakness of the immune system, The world syndrome is used to emphasise that AIDS presents itself as a group of signs and symptoms and not a single disease. AIDS cannot be diagnosed on the existence of one sign or symptom. All the symptoms of AIDS can be symptoms of other disease too. Therefore, a person cannot tell whether he/she has AIDS or not unless he/she has been examined at a hospital or health centre and diagnosed as such.

Viruses are tiny organism that causes many diseases. Human diseases caused by viruses include measles polio, mumps, common cold and flu. Viruses cannot multiply on their own. They can only reproduce themselves by using the genetic materials of the cells of the host animals or plant. In order to reproduce HIV attaches itself to the genetic material for human cell it has infected. This makes it very hard for either the body or drugs to deal with it, without destroying the cell itself. This is why it has been difficult to develop a 'cure' for HIV so far, since anything damages the virus is likely to also damage the cell it has infected. The destruction of the immune system by the virus means infectious organism can invade the body unchallenged and multiply to cause disease.

HIV causes damage to the immune system. The immune system is the means by which the body protects itself from infection and disease. The skin serves as a physical barrier and the white cells in our blood deals with potentially harmful organism such as viruses and bacteria. HIV is attracted to white blood cells. These cells are among the most important in working of body's immune system, as they regulate the immune response of the body in case of an infection.

After being infected with HIV, the body produces the antibodies to HIV in an effort to protect itself. These antibodies are not powerful enough to neutralise the virus and by this time HIV will have already attached itself to and integrated in to the genetic material of some white blood cells, ready to reproduce itself some time in the future. Most people with HIV show no symptoms of disease and may be a symptomatic for months and even up to ten years. These people may remain completely healthy and free from symptoms of disease but they have the virus in their blood and are at risk of developing. AIDS at any time in future. Once a person is infected with HIV he/she can transmit the virus to other people even through he/she may appear perfectly healthy and may not known that he/she has been infected with HIV.

There is no way to knowing whether a person is infected with HIV expect by having a blood test. Some people with the HIV infection develop one or more of the signs of symptoms, which make up AIDS. These can be easily mistaken for those of many other illnesses. They include persistent fatigue, severe weight loss. Night sweats or fevers lasting several weeks, persistent diarrhoea lasting over one month. Common complaints of people with AIDS are painless swollen grants, usually in the neck and armpits, which last for at least three months. Some people develop recurrent infections such as oral thrust (Candida), Herpes zoster (shingles) or genital Herpes. Many develop TB. A common manifestation in children is failure to thrive, prolonged diarrhoea and pneumonia which do not respond to treatment.

These symptoms are also common in people who do not have HIV infection. However, when several of these occur at the same time and they are persistent, this may indicate the development of AIDS. As the immune system is increasingly damaged, these health problems become more serious and more difficult to treat, as the body no longer responds to treatment.

11.3.1.1. Transmission of HIV

Sexual intercourse

The most common route to transmission is unprotected sexual intercourse with an infected partner. It accounts for nearly 80 percent of the world's HIV infections. HIV is present in semen and in cervical and vaginal fluids and the vagina and penis provide entry points to the body. The rapid spread of HIV/AIDS in the world is attributed to transmission through sex. HIV has been described as the 'latest' Sexually Transmitted Disease. Transmission is made easier by the presence of other STDs, particularly genital ulcer disease such as chancroid and syphilis. In presence of an STD, particularly where a sore is present, the risk of contracting HIV during unprotected sex with an infected person is very high. This is because semen or vaginal secretions of an HIV infected person can come in contact with open sores easily.

Infected mother to new-born child

HIV can be transmitted by a woman with HIV to her child before, during birth and after birth. Before birth, it may be transmitted across the placenta to the foetus and during birth it may be transmitted through mother's blood. The chance of an infected mother passing on HIV to her child is estimated at about 30 percent. That means one out of every three children born to an infected mother is likely to be born already infected with HIV. Few children with HIV survive for longer than 2-3 years.

Blood

Human blood provides a good medium for the growth of micro-organism including HIV because of its nutrient value, adequate oxygen content and adequate temperature. Therefore, infusion of blood and blood products, which are infected with HIV, is one of the most efficient means of transmission of HIV infection. As such testing of blood for HIV before transfusion is mandatory. This means that before transfusion each and every unit of blood must be tested for HIV. National AIDS Control Organisation in India is, therefore, trying to provide facilities of testing of every unit of blood.

As a virus which lives in the blood, HIV may be transmitted by the transfusion of blood from an infected donor. HIV can also be transmitted through the use without proper sterilisation of needles, syringes, blades, knives, surgical instruments and other piercing instrument that have been used on an infected person. This includes the instruments used for circumcision, tattooing, acupuncture, ear piercing and traditional healing practices. Used needles and syringes can be soiled with minute amounts of left over blood. If these needles and syringes are used, then the infected blood could directly transfer HIV in to the blood stream. It is should be noted that the possibility of transmission of HIV through normal injections in clinics and hospitals is extremely low. Sharing of syringes among injecting drug users is common. Such a behaviour is highly risky from the point of the view of getting HIV infection as injecting drugs users often end up giving themselves mini transfusion.

Sexually transmitted diseases

STDs are those diseases, which are transferred via mucous membranes and sections of the sexual organs, throat and rectum. Most STDs are easy to treat. It they are detected and treated early, they do not cause any serious problems. If they are not detected and treated early, they do not detected and treated early, the infection may spread and cause complications such as sterility. They are relatively easy to contract, and so it is important to know what they are, what they look like and what you need to do to get them treated.

In India, there is a very high incidents of STDs, primarily because contrary to popular belief many people in the country have sex with multiple partners. In addition to this there is lack of knowledge of STDs, inadequate health facilities, inadequate utilisation of health facilities, due to stigma associated with STDs and urbanisation, which at times, compels the person to leave his/her spouse and family in villages. Limited condom use and lack of personal hygiene are other factors.

HIV infection/AIDS is also a kind of sexually transmitted disease, the significant difference being that while most of the other STDs can be cured, HIV/AIDS is incurable. The incidence of HIV/AIDS is found to be directly co-related to the incidence of other sexually transmitted diseases, so people at low risk of STDS are also at low risk of HIV. For this reason too, it is important to concentrate on the prevention and treatment of STDs. The life style, which prevents STDs will also prevent HIV.

Prevention of STDs infection: Abstinence from all sexual activity is the most effective prevention. However, most people do not choose a lifetime abstinence. The risk of acquiring an STD, including HIV is virtually absent when one has sexual intercourse with a mutually faithful monogamous uninfected partner. In all other situations condoms should be used for protection against infections. Personal hygiene (washing of genitals after intercourse) might also contribute to prevention of infection, but by itself this is less effective than condom use.

Signs and Symptoms of STDs : All STDs will not have signs and symptoms and the same STD may seem different in different people. It is extremely important to note that many women and some men have an STD without sign or symptom. The following signs could indicate presence of STD in a sexually active person:

Women: An unusual discharge or smell from vagina. Pain in the pelvic area between the navel and sex organs. Burning or itching around the vagina. Bleeding from the vagina which is not the menstrual flow. Pain inside the vagina when having sex. Swelling in the groin- area around the sex organ.

A person may be infected for some time and not know it. The danger is that the person can spread the disease to others without realising it. It is important that sexually transmitted diseases are adequately treated. If not, they can become chronic and be the case of serious complications. For adequate and effective treatment it is necessary to go to a qualified doctor. Self treatment or treatment by quacks is not advisable. One should not fell ashamed to go to a doctor. It is the doctor's duty to maintain strict confidentiality.

11.3.1.2. Prevention and Control of HIV/AIDS

There is no preventive vaccine or cure. The only option available is to prevent it by observing practices that are safe compliance with such practices can make a significant difference. The discussion in the following pages, therefore, is focused on the preventive practices regarding three major routes of HIV infection: Sexual Intercourse; Blood; and Mother to Child.

Sexual intercourse

In the most cases, HIV infection is caused by unsafe sex practices. A healthy attitude towards sex and observing responsible sexual behaviour can produce the changes of getting HIV infection. Abstinence from sex, sticking to one uninfected life partner and not having multiple relations (or not having pre-material and extra-material sexual relations) constitute responsible sexual behaviour which are the best guarantees against HIV/AIDS.

Use of condoms

Sex plays a very important role in a person's growth in to adulthood and in his/her subsequent life. Decisions regarding sex must be based on careful and mature consideration: References to sexual behaviour have been made only in the context of HIV/AIDS. The use of condoms is recommended not only for avoiding unwanted pregnancy but also as a 'protection' against HIV/AIDS and other STDs. Although the use of condom provides good protection, it should be remembered that it does not make sex 100 percent safe.

Blood

Blood Safety: The Blood Safety programme is an integral part of the AIDS Control programme. In India there are more than 1000 blood banks, both government and non government, which collect and supply blood. HIV Zonal blood testing centres have been set up in many cities and towns of the country. The centres receive samples of blood from blood banks for HIV testing. Under the drug and cosmetics Act, it is mandatory to test every unit of blood for HIV. The Zonal blood testing centres and district level blood banks have been provided with testing kits and the necessary equipment for conducting tests. The blood of a donor is discarded if it is tested HIV positive. In order to know the prevalence and progression of HIV in the community and the country as a whole, the mechanism of sentinel surveillance has been established. This is being done through screening of the blood samples, collected from sentinel sites including STD clinics, antenatal clinics, drug de-addition clinics, etc, the surveillance date from different states is complied at the national level. Efforts are also being made to augment voluntary blood donations and to phase out professional donors.

Mother to child

The risk of an HIV infected mother passing the virus to her unborn child is about 30% the risk being greater if she has symptoms of AIDS rather than if she has no symptoms. The risk of passing HIV through breast-milk is relatively small. Breast-milk has many substances in it that protect an infant's health and the benefits of breast-feeding for mother and child are well recognised. Bottle-feeding is not safe because of difficulties in sterilising the feeding bottles or lack of clean water supplies. In developing countries, the risk of an infant becoming infected through breast-feeding is usually outweighed by the benefits of breast-feeding.

11.3.1.3. Drug Abuse and HIV Vulnerability

The Asia including India has a long history of traditional use of locally produced drugs, such as cannabis and opium. In recent years the region has become a transit point for the international drug trafficking. Drug abuse is on the increase, and so are the problem caused by this abuse. It causes not only the deterioration in the family life and violence. In more recent years the lifestyle and risky behaviour of drug users are also linked to the HIV/AIDS pandemic.

In India the abuse of heroin was confined to smoking and inhaling until about 1993. At that time the practice of injecting heroin began to increase. Today, it is a major concern in several parts of the country, especially Urban centres like Mumbai and Delhi and the North- Eastern states bordering Myanmar which together with Loas and Thailand constitute the Golden Triangle. The worst aspect of the drug abuse is its deepest impression on the school and college going youth who is most vulnerable. Most drug users begin taking drugs at an early age, as adolescents or even younger. Young students take to drugs due to peer pressure, curiosity, ignorance, changing social structure, urbanisation and other related causes.

11.3.2. Teachers Role as AIDS Educators

While traditionally psychologists, social workers and doctors have served as counsellors, it is important to explore the role of teachers as AIDS educators with young students. What a teacher needs to do is to gain the trust and confidence of students.

Responsible sexual behaviour being an important component of AIDS education, a teacher has to function as a resource for accurate information in matters relating to sex and sexuality which are sensitive in nature. Many teachers find it difficult to get over their embarrassment and shyness while dealing with such issues. With training, the embarrassment and shyness can be overcome among the teachers and they can be in a better position to communicate with the students in their own language and appreciate their problems and needs. The advice given by the teacher is more acceptable to students with a higher possibility of behaviour change.

It is extremely important for teachers to be non-judgemental so that he/she can treat the student as a person needing understanding, compassion and care. In communicating about AIDS/STD, understanding, compassion and care are very important for bringing about desirable change. The teacher should not put off a student when he/she asks questions. Teacher should not tell the students that their questions are silly but rather tell them that their questions are very genuine and relevant.

The teacher may try to answer a student's questions as best as he/she can. For personal problems too the teacher may advise the student to the best of his/her ability. At the same time, if the problems demand, the student should be advised to consult a qualified doctor/counsellor for further treatment/counselling. The student should also be advised to talk to his/her parents in case of any serious personal problems.

11.4. Conclusion

Education is a vital aspect of population change, social development and economic growth for every society, impacting the economic future and social well-being of all individuals. Education is also a globally recognised human right.

Education provides enormous impetus to the development of the poorer countries of the world, by providing opportunities for individuals, especially women, to achieve their potential and contribute meaningfully to their communities. Education not only imparts technical information - reading, writing, mathematics, sciences - but provides opportunities for self-discovery and personal enrichment. This knowledge and increased understanding of their place in the world and their community empower individuals to more effectively realise their desires and achieve their potentials. Through education, individuals are better able to enjoy healthy lifestyles, achieve the desired number and spacing of children, undertake the type of work that they wish to undertake and, in sum, better manage their lives. When aggregated, these individual choices, decisions and improvements have powerful effects on national development. No society can consider itself truly developed without its citizens' are being educated.

References

Bain, I., "Southeast Asia, International Migration, Quarterly Review", *special edition on Migration and HIV/AIDS*, Vol 36:4, 1998.

Caouette, T et al., "Assessment of Reproductive and Sexual Health", *Concerns and Realities of Migrant Workers in Burma and Thailand (Draft),* Institute for Population and Social Science Research, Mahidol University, Thailand, 1999.

Family Health International, "Making Prevention Work: No.10. Crossing Borders - Reaching Mobile Population at Risk", May, 1999.

Fernandez I., "Migration and HIV/AIDS", *In: 4th International Congress on AIDS in Asia and the Pacific in Manila*, October 1997.

Geust, P., "Overview of the Population Mobility Situation in Asia and its Implications for HIV/AIDS", *paper presented at the Fifth International Congress on AIDS in Asia and the Pacific*, Kuala Lumpur, 20-27 October, 1999.

Hsu, L.-N. and J. d. Guerny, "Population Movement, Development and HIV/AIDS: Looking Towards the Future", Bangkok, *UNDP & FAO*, 2000.

Kaldor, J. et al., ed., "HIV surveillance in hard-to-reach populations", *AIDS* 15 (Suppl. 3), April 2001.

Kelly P., "Managing HIV Vulnerability of Mobile Populations: Methodologies for Data Collection", *In: Satellite Symposium, 4th International Congress on AIDS in Asia and the Pacific in Manila.* October 1997

Kerrigan, D., *Peer Education and HIV/AIDS: Concepts, Uses and Challenges,* Washington, DC: HORIZONS/Population Council, 1999

Lamptey, P., "Reducing heterosexual transmission of HIV in poor countries", *British Medical Journal,* 324:207–211 2002.

Livi-Bacci, Massimo, *Population and Nutrition: An Essay on European Demographic History,* Cambridge: Cambridge University Press, 1991.

McKeown, Thomas, *The Origins of Human Disease,* Oxford: Basil Blackwell, 1988.

Nguyen T H., *Population Redistribution Policy and Migration Trends in Vietnam: Past, Present and Future,* 1998.

Prah Ruger J., "Combating HIV/AIDS in developing countries", *British Medical Journal,* 2004.

Skeldon R., "Population Mobility and HIV Vulnerability in South East Asia: An Assessment and Analysis", *UNDP Southeast Asia HIV and Development Project,* February, 2000.

UNAIDS, "Migration and AIDS", *International Migration,* Vol. 36 (4): 445-468, 1998.

........., "Migration and HIV/AIDS", *Program Coordination Board Second Ad hoc Thematic Meeting,* New Delhi, December, 1998.

UNDP, "Reduction of HIV Vulnerability within the Land Transport Sector", *UNDP-SEA HIV Development Project,* 2000.

UNICEF, "Mobile Populations and HIV Vulnerability: Approaches to Applied Research", Bangkok, UNICEF, UNAIDS, 1998.

CHAPTER 12

Population Education in Schools and Colleges

12.1. Introduction

A curriculum means the total situation (or all situations) selected and organised by the institutions and made available to the teacher to operate and translate the ultimate aim of education into reality. Curriculum does not mean only the academic subjects traditionally taught in the school but it includes the totality of experiences that a pupil receives through the manifold activities that go on in the school, in the class room, library, laboratory, workshop, playground and numerous informal contacts between teachers and pupils. Thus the term curriculum, in its broad sense, refers to all the planned learning activities or experiences provided by an educational programme to a group of learners or target audience. As such it may include objectives, content, learning activities, materials, teaching aids and evaluation means and tools. In its narrow sense a curriculum may refer solely to the core contents or content outline of a particular programme or field.

Curriculum development is the most important component of an educational innovation, namely, Population Education. The introduction of population issues in the school curriculum, the explanation of the inter-relationships between a wide range of social phenomena both at micro and the macro levels, the explicit attention to the preparation of students for their future role as adult decision makers in their families, the community and the nation. This innovation can have an impact on curriculum design and instruction and make it possible to assert that population education can become both a stimulus to and a support for wide-spread educational reform. It is through the curricular materials that the future citizens receive population education messages. It aims at the development of awareness and attitudes that will make learners to develop responsible behaviour in the context of population issues.

12.2. Population Education in Schools

The onus of meeting the challenge of population growth rests on the young people who will constitute the adult population in the coming two to three decades. It is their reproductive behaviour when they become adults, which is going to affect considerably the population situation in future. In order to achieve population stabilisation, the future parents, who are most important segment of society, must be involved. Their changed attitude towards family size is vital. Population education through the school system could be a potent instrument for developing these attitudes and competencies among this group and help them to take a rational decision. Different people have different opinion about the introduction of population education at different grade levels. Some of the arguments given for the introduction of population education at the elementary stage in India are as follows:

(i) Elementary stage has the highest enrolment. Children drop-out as they go up higher in the educational ladder. Introducing population education at this stage will benefit larger number of children.

(ii) Elementary school curriculum generally provides flexibility for introducing new concerns. Since there is no public examination at this stage, a greater number of opportunities for the use of experimental materials are available.

(iii) A number of research studies have indicated that it is easy to bring about change in attitudes at this formative stage.

(iv) Primary school teachers still play an important role in the rural areas. Their exposure to population related issues will help both students and the community at large in changing their attitude and behaviour in a right direction.

Those who argue for the introduction of population education at the secondary level give the following reasons:

(i) Students at this stage are in the process of growing up. These are the students who are already or will be taking decisions regarding marriage and reproductive behaviour very shortly. Education in matters related to adolescent reproductive health and other population related issues is of immediate relevance.

ii) Students at this stage can grasp and understand population issues in greater depth.

(iii) The number of teachers to be trained in population education is comparatively smaller.

It would be better if population education is introduced at all the stages of school education. Efforts should be made to reach even those who are not in the school.

12.3. Curriculum Development Approaches

The following two approaches are being followed in most of the countries, for the development of curriculum in population education. One approach is Separate Subject approach and the other is Integrated Approach.

12.3.1. Separate Subject Approach

In the first approach, population education becomes a subject area along with other subjects taught at one or more grade levels. A separate subject affords the greatest possibility of systematic and sustained learning. Some countries have started thinking of introducing population education as a separate subject at the secondary level. For example, Philippines and Thailand are offering it as a separate elective course at secondary level. Although this approach is much effective and the chances of dilution and diffusion are less but it has not been put into practice in most of the countrie as Population Education is multi-disciplinary in nature and draws its content from various subjects. Secondly, school time tables are already over crowded and teachers find it difficult to accommodate a new course. Thirdly, new teachers will be required if it is introduced as a separate course. Most of the countries have, therefore, used an integrated approach to include population education concepts in different school subjects.

12.3.2. Integrated Approach

Separate population education course or a series of courses to be included at elementary and secondary stages is not the most appropriate way to develop the necessary awareness. The curriculum is already crowded, the demand from the traditional disciplines generally reduced the possibility of adding a new population course. Further children will learn better if they are confronted with population related issues both throughout their school curriculum and during their entire period of schooling". Population education is multi disciplinary in nature and related to various subject/areas. The National Seminar on Population Education held at Bombay in 1969 also recommended "Population Education should be introduced into the curriculum of schools and colleges by including it in so far as it may be possible, in the areas of study such as Social Studies, Sciences, Health Education, Mathematics, Languages etc. In fact this serninar was of the view that it may be possible to achieve all the objectives in view by including population education suitably in the curricula of appropriate subjects already included in the curriculum."

Integration of population education in different school subjects can be possible in two ways:

i) *Unit Approach*: In this approach new units relating to population education are developed and added to the existing units in the course/syllabus of the subject area. This type of approach is adopted in countries like Philippines, the Republic of Korea and Thailand. The subjects usually chosen for the inclusion of population education units are Social Sciences, General Sciences, Biology, Mathematics, Home Economics, Health Education, Physical Education and Geography;

ii) *Infusion Approach*: This approach implies inclusion of population education concepts and data into the normal process of instruction throughout the curriculum without having to develop separate course of new units. Inclusion of this type involves enriching and expanding the existing unit in the syllabi of the accommodating subject areas to include population education related ideas. In this approach examples can be substituted into the already existing materials by population related examples. Through the substitution of examples, education content remains the same, only the substance of the example changes. This infusion was done either by incorporating in the textbooks or by publishing them in teacher guides. In other words, infusion with existing subject of population education concept means that no major curriculum reorganisation is necessary. Time table need not be disturbed and existing teachers can teach with very little training.

This approach has also some demerits. In this approach, there is danger of fragmentation of the programme and the consequent failure of the pupil to attain the kind of understanding that the programme requires. It is much easier to see integration on paper than it is to achieve it in the reality of the school situation. It has been observed that population education concepts tend to be lost in the process of integration and the whole purpose of population education gets diffused.

In India efforts have been made to develop and integrate a few separate lessons as well as to infuse some ideas in the syllabi and textbooks of various subject areas at different school stages.

12.4. Population Education Conceptual Framework

The concept of Population Education has relatively a short history. Ever since its inception, it has been changing and evolving at relatively faster pace. This has been so primarily because its central subject—the population phenomenon—has been unfolding itself in quick succession and identifying new dimensions of its interrelationships with other facets of human development.

In India, Population Education was first conceptualised during the later half of nineteen sixties. The National Seminar on Population Education held in 1969 defined it as an education to make learner aware of the causes and effects of population changes.

The concept of Population Education was reoriented to become value laden as population issues are predominantly value-laden. By early 1990 again a need was felt to reconceputalise Population Education. The feedback received through in-built monitoring and findings of evaluation studies identified two basic limitations.

The Core Curricular areas emphasised in the National Policy of Education, 1986, such as Observance of Small Family Norm, Equality of Sexes, Protection of Environment, Removal of Social Barriers and Inculcation of Scientific Temper were also to be reflected. The basic change in the perception of population development inter-relationship reflected in the ICPD Programme of Action registered a Paradigm Shift and put forth a fresh population agenda for the nations. The experiences gained during the implementation of NPEP in India also highlighted the gap regarding some crucial areas concerning sex-related matters, HIV/AIDS and Drug Abuse.

12.5. Curriculum Development and Objectives of Population Education

The process of curriculum development should take into consideration the following objectives of population education:

- Making learners aware of the inter-relationships between population and sustainable development.
- Developing in them an understanding of the criticality of essential conditions of population stabilisation for better quality of life of present and future generations.
- Inculcating in them rational attitude and responsible behaviour towards population and development issues.
- Making them understand the crucial aspects of adolescent reproductive health, focusing on the elements of process of growing up, and implication of HIV/AIDS and Drug Abuse.
- Inculcating in them rational attitude towards sex and drugs and promoting respect for the opposite sex; and
- Empowering them to take informed decisions on issues of population and development including reproductive health.

12.5.1. Identification of Population Education Contents

Population Education is a value-laden concept. Its content is culture and region specific and inter-disciplinary in nature. The desirability of having need-based as well as a demand based curriculum calls for a serious exercise in respect of selecting appropriate and relevant contents.

12.5.2. Curriculum Transaction

The changes reflected in the Conceptual Framework of Population Education will require identification and adoption of suitable strategies of curriculum transaction. The strategy of integration of population education contents into the syllabi and textbooks of selected subjects at the school level has been adopted. The textbooks are considered effective instruments for exposing students to population education ideas and messages that are essential for making their understanding of population phenomena better. In this context the following strategies may be useful:

(i) Attempt has to be made to include only those contents that could receive comprehensive and effective treatment in the syllabi and textbooks of concerned subjects. Those natural entry points be selected that have potentiality of providing comprehensive treatment to relevant population education contents. The most crucial aspect of effective integration would be to integrate maximum contents at minimum points in most comprehensive way. Only those subjects should be given priority that have greater potentiality to incorporate these contents.

(ii) Some contents of population education may not find suitable entry into the existing syllabi and textbooks because of the limitation of the subject areas. For such contents supplementary reading materials and 'audio-visual materials may be developed. Classroom teaching needs to be supplemented by a variety of co-curricular activities such as project assignments, play way activities, demonstration, group discussion, painting, essay writing, debate, elocution, question box, quiz competition, etc.

(iii) Any curriculum remains a futile exercise unless it is put into practice. Teacher occupies an important place in the implementation of this area. It is the teacher who has to use the material, create learning situations in the classroom for their students and help them to learn. Their orientation to the new curriculum is, therefore, absolutely essential. Both in-service and pre-service orientation should be organised. The teacher should be fed with suitable instructional materials like teacher's guide, handbooks with update information and audio-visual materials.

Population education taught by an imaginative teacher could enable students to creative thinking and action in relation to a number of problems and issues that surround them. Problem solving/discovery approach and value clarification approaches are regarded to be more functional.

(iv)The population education contents integrated in different subject areas, other materials developed for promoting effective integration, teacher training organised and activities conducted in schools should be evaluated to find out whether the desired outcomes in terms of awareness and attitude have been achieved. Being value-laden, continuous and comprehensive evaluation should be followed so that necessary improvements are made in the curriculum and materials and its transaction.

12.6. Demography and Education

The relationship between education and demography has been described and analysed extensively in a great deal of research work. While it affects population dynamics, this in turn affects education latter, which is now considered a key variable in education planning across the board. Education has been shown to have an influence on the mortality level. Indeed, more educated people have a greater chance of survival and, hence, longer life expectancy. They are more aware of the rules of hygiene and less fatalistic in the face of disease.

A correlation also exists between education and marriage. Educated people marry later in life than those with little or no schooling. The link here is slightly more complex, however, and varies according to gender. Among men and women with an equal level of education, for example, men have a higher probability to get married earlier than women.

Levels of education seem to have an impact on migration patterns. It is the more educated people who tend to migrate to cities or abroad. That said, there is no clear-cut causal relationship. Schooling only goes part of the way to explaining rural to urban migration, the main reasons being job opportunities and income differences.

The relationship between education and fertility has, perhaps, been studied more than any other by researchers around the world. It, too, is complex in nature, and hinges on the influence of intermediate factors such as marital patterns. Education not only raises the age at marriage but it also changes the value systems, leading individuals to desire small families. In societies where most fertility occurs within marital unions an educated woman who marries later in life will also start having babies later. As a result she will have fewer children than a woman with little or no education.

Determined to find a job, striving for independence and with more diversified centres of interest, qualified women are more acutely aware of the conflict between bringing up children and having time to themselves. Another baby means an increasing "opportunity cost". Educated women will therefore reign in their desire to have large numbers of children. Women who have been educated will want the same for their children, and prefer to have fewer children so as to guarantee them a better education. Educated women also have a higher social status and tend, more often than not, to be urban residents. Finally, they know more about contraception. All of these factors affecting fertility are, in fact, relatively inextricably intertwined.

Demography is especially important in the realm of education planning, with population statistics serving as the basis upon which to develop education plans. The structure or age composition of the population determines the size of the school-age population, i.e. the potential demand for education, which is clearly the starting point for any education policy. The proportion of school-age children in most developing countries is very high, bringing enormous pressure to bear on traditional education systems. Density and geographic distribution-which hinge both on fertility rates that can vary depending on the region and on migratory flows-affect education costs, choice of school types, and their size and location.

The pace and dynamics of population growth, mainly determined by birth rates, is crucial to education planning. Indeed, the number of future births will affect the number of pupils or students to be accommodated at every level of the education system each year and, hence, on the rate of construction of new educational infrastructure. A fall in the number of pupils due to falling birth rates or to migration is just as important to planners. Such patterns can lead to a policy shift in regard to school closure or redeployment.

12.7. Changes in the School-age Population

High rates population growth in the past are still influencing the number of children to be enrolled in the world, in spite of a significant decrease in fertility. The world's total primary school-age population, for example, grew from around 600 million in 1990 to 648 million in 2000, and looks set to reach an estimated 701 million by 2015, that is, 100 million more than in 1990. These figures show the scale of the efforts that the world will need to make to meet the potential demand for education and ensure that all school-age children are enrolled by 2015. The picture, however, varies depending on the region. While other regions will see a decrease in the size of their school-age populations in the future, due to significant falls in fertility, sub-Saharan Africa, South and West Asia and the region encompassing the Arab States are likely to see a rise in the number of children to be enrolled.

Sub-Saharan Africa has recorded the largest increase in this age group: up from 84 million in 1990 to 106 million in 2000, an average of 2.6 per cent per annum. Despite a slowdown in the pace of that growth, mainly due to the region's ongoing fertility transition, the school-age population is still set to rise to an estimated 140 million by 2015. Demand for education there will remain far greater than in the other regions of the world, exacerbating the problems in achieving universal access to education in a region where resources are scarce. This is equally true, albeit to a lesser degree, of South and West Asia and certain Arab countries, where fertility remains high.

12.7.1. Primary School-age Population

In East Asia and the Pacific, on the other hand, where the average enrolment ratio is about 94 per cent, the decrease in the school-age population will facilitate the achievement of UPE. In countries where all children are already in school (Australia, Japan, Malaysia, the Republic of Korea, North America, Western Europe and certain countries in Latin America and the Caribbean), the decrease in the school-age population makes it possible to release resources to improve the quality of primary education and also to develop access to other levels of education.

Comparison between different countries and regions shows that while demographic trends may play an important role in the development of education, but their impact depends on interaction with other socio-economic, cultural and political factors. In the 1990s, for example, some countries managed to expand children's access to school in spite of high population growth. These countries include Malawi, Laos, Uganda and Kenya, where the increase in enrolment has mainly been due to a political will to achieve the goal of UPE. In countries where high population growth often goes hand-in-hand with low enrolment levels, demographic trends-which can have a negative impact on the state of education-represent a factor that absolutely must be taken into account in any strategy aimed at achieving UPE. Indeed, because high population growth risks hindering the development of education, it may prevent the role of education in facilitating the demographic transition and improving people's health and well-being. Where there is high population growth, UPE strategies must coexist with population programmes that tend to reduce fertility. They are not interchangeable but, given the mutual relationship between education and demography, they are complementary.

12.7.2. Need for Population Education

While demographic statistics may serve as the underpinnings of education plans, enabling planners to reckon with the ways in which population growth could hinder achievement of the goal of UPE, it should also be stressed that population education is a key aspect of population policies and programmes whose aim is to bring population growth under control. The ICPD Plan of Action recommends education about population issues which, to be most effective, must begin in primary school and continue through all levels of formal and non-formal education taking into account the rights and responsibilities of parents and the needs of children and adolescents. What is population education? In a nutshell, population education can be seen as an instructional or educational process addressing the relationship between demographic trends and individual and family welfare. Originally devised as an educational response to contemporary population issues and problems, the aim of population education is to help families and communities understand how their demographic characteristics affect every aspect of their daily lives. As such, it empowers the individual to make rational and well-thought decisions on population issues and, hence, to help improve his or her own socio-economic and cultural wellbeing together with that of his or her family, community, country or even the world.

Content-wise, population education stands at the crossroads between several different disciplines often associated with development: demography, sociology, anthropology, education, history, geography, biology, economics, medicine, and so on. Population education therefore incorporates an integrative approach combining micro-level analyses and macro-level analyses on the nature and consequences of the population's behaviour. It also uses integrative methods embracing environmental education, family life education and sex education.

Efforts to expand access to education have coincided with an extraordinary growth in population numbers. No century had witnessed on investment from female education is reduced. Overall, however, women receive a higher return on investment in schooling than men do. As regards social returns, with few exceptions recent studies have confirmed the significant positive association between schooling, and productivity and economic growth. Other studies have looked at the positive spillover effects beyond education's impact on the growth of gross domestic product (GDP)—effects that are not normally taken into account. The greater productivity of individual workers has also been found to enhance the productivity of co-workers, while higher levels of worker education facilitate the discovery, adaptation and use of more efficient production processes.

For low-income countries, primary education was the best investment, while in middle-income countries, where primary education already tends to be more widely available, increased investment in secondary education yielded the highest social returns. Among high-income countries, returns were greatest for tertiary education. This suggests that in low-income settings, primary education deserves priority in the allocation of resources. Based on such evidence, many countries have misallocated spending between education subsectors, with a disproportionate share of resources going to secondary and university education. Other studies have investigated the role of primary education in reducing poverty and income inequality. The overwhelming conclusion of these studies was that primary education is a potent means of reducing poverty and inequality, with particularly marked benefits for the poorest segments of society.

A number of other benefits from investments in education and training have been identified. For example, studies have found that primary education contributes to better natural resource management, and more rapid technological adaptation and innovation; and that education is linked with the greater diffusion of information, which is crucial for boosting productivity.

Studies of the relationship have often found effects that were not statistically significant, but when effects were significant, children in large families usually had lower educational participation and attainment. Results suggest that this relationship is weak in comparison with the relationship between amount of education and other factors household poverty, for instance that independently affect children's schooling. The relationship between family size and investment in children has been found to vary according to level of development, phase of the demographic transition, level of government social expenditures and cultural factors. In some countries, unwanted births have been found to reduce educational attainment and to be a major reason that girls drop out of school.

12.7.3. School Enrolment and Educational Attainment

In the nine years following the World Conference on Education for All, between 1990 and 1999, both primary and secondary school enrolments grew at over one and a half times the pace of increase observed during the 1980s. World total enrolment at the primary level increased from 597 million in 1990 to 683 million in 1999. This growth took place exclusively in the developing world. Worldwide enrolment in secondary education grew by 103 million between 1990 and 1999, and developing countries accounted for over 90 per cent of the increase.

Gross and net enrolment ratios are the main measures of participation in education. Because enrolment may be quite different from actual attendance and completion, however, these statistics need to be considered in conjunction with other educational indicators. The net enrolment ratio (NER) refers to the enrolment of the official age group for a given level of education expressed as a percentage of the corresponding population. The gross enrolment ratio (GER) refers to the total enrolment in a specific level of education, regardless of age, expressed as a percentage of the official school-age population corresponding to the same level of education. Repetition is considered to be an important aspect of both the quality of education and, along with school survival, of the internal efficiency of the education system. Furthermore, high repetition rates often point to high dropout rates. The percentage of repeaters is fairly high in many developing countries. More than 10 per cent of pupils repeat a grade of primary education in more than half of the countries in sub-Saharan Africa.

12.7.4. Adult Illiteracy Rates

Over the 30-year period between 1970 and 2000, estimated adult illiteracy rates (for ages 15 years or over) declined worldwide from 37 to 20 percent, mostly owing to effects of increases in primary school enrolments. By 2015, adult illiteracy is projected to decrease further to 15 per cent. Even though there has been substantial progress in all regions, illiteracy remains common in much of the developing world. In 2000, about one fourth of the adults in the developing regions, and almost half in the least developed countries, were illiterate. The level was 45 per cent in South and West Asia and 40 per cent both in sub-Saharan Africa and in the Arab States and North Africa, but under 15 per cent in Eastern Asia and Oceania and in Latin America and the Caribbean.

Despite the worldwide gains observed in literacy rates, the number of adult illiterates remains very high and almost constant because of the impact of population growth. In 1990, some 879 million adults in the world were illiterate; by the year 2000, their number is estimated to have declined only slightly, to 862 million. Among the developing regions, the number of illiterate adults increased between 1990 and 2000 in sub-Saharan Africa, in the Arab States and North Africa and in South and West Asia, and by 2000 these regions accounted for about 70 per cent of the world's adult illiterate population. Without major changes, these regions will hold 80 per cent of the world's illiterate population by 2015. In a predominantly literate society, there is intense social pressure for all to learn to read and write. Correspondingly, in a predominately illiterate society, there is likely to be less pressure for those who cannot read and write to achieve literacy.

Disparities between girls' and boys' enrolment are usually lower when only children of regular school age are taken into account using net enrolment than when gross enrolment is examined. It appears that although more boys are enrolled overall, they also make up more of the population of over-age pupils. In the majority of countries, boys also repeat grades more than girls.

For secondary education, countries that have moderate gender disparities in favour of males have a reasonable chance of reaching parity by the goal date of 2005, but in countries with high disparities in favour of boys, the goal of achieving gender parity in primary and secondary education by 2005 seems unlikely to be reached, and even more unlikely for countries with a GPI below 0.60. As is the case for primary education, most of these countries are from Central and West Africa and are members of the group of least developed countries. It will take strong and innovative approaches, integrating the economic, social and cultural dimensions of gender inequity, to redress the situation.

In general, gender disparities in education are higher at the level of the adult population than for children currently attending school. However, a trend towards lower gender literacy gaps can be observed in all regions of the world. For the developing regions taken together, the gender gap in illiteracy declined 18 percentage points in 1990 to 15 in 2000 and is projected to fall to 10 in 2015. With the exception of Latin America and the Caribbean, however, where the gap is almost closed, in all other developing regions women remain disproportionately disadvantaged in terms of literacy.

12.7.5. Gender Disparities

The gender balance of entrants to primary education provides an early indicator of the success or failure of efforts to narrow the gender gap in education. Globally, 49 per cent of those at school-age entry (age 6) are girls. However, during the 1990s, the actual proportion of girls among new entrants was about 46 per cent. The share of girls among new entrants ranges from 44 per cent in South and West Asia to 49 per cent in Latin America and the Caribbean. In the period between 1990/91 and 1999/2000, gender disparities narrowed in some countries with the biggest gaps, indicating that measures to improve gender equality taken during the 1990s were bringing results. The gender parity index (GPI) is the ratio of the enrolment ratio for girls to that for boys. Based on gross enrolment ratios, the GPI in both primary and secondary school enrolment in the more developed countries is near or slightly above one, indicating higher enrolment ratios for girls than boys. However, in most developing countries, a substantial gender gap in enrolment in favour of boys remains at both the primary and secondary levels of education.

12.7.6. Educational Quality

Several EFA goals mention the need for an education of good quality. The most appropriate framework would be one that covered the inputs, processes, and outputs of the education system. Many of the existing EFA indicators cover inputs into the educational system, at least as far as numbers of students are concerned. Other inputs that require measurement might include textbooks, school buildings and other facilities. Process indicators measure the way in which the inputs are turned into outputs. The most widely used process indicator in education is the pupil-to-teacher ratio. This is normally seen as an indicator of class size.

Regarding outcome indicators, international tests of student achievement are becoming more common in almost all regions of the world. They can provide robust comparable data for a whole region, though, often, access to this data is limited, and there can be reluctance to permit such comparisons to be made. These tests are expensive and are likely to be carried out only among the larger and more affluent developing countries.

12.7.7. Education and Entry into Reproductive Life

Timing of marriage, onset of sexual relationships and first birth are influenced by both cultural norms and socio-economic factors. Where education is a prerequisite for obtaining desirable jobs and achieving social mobility, the opportunity cost of early marriage or pregnancy can be significant. Yet, even as schooling deters young women and men from early marriage, education also gives them a level of independence that may lead to early onset of sexual relations and childbearing. On the other hand, in societies where there are few incentives for prolonged schooling and limited alternatives to marriage, young women and men are more likely to marry at relatively early ages.

Education plays a greater role in delaying marriage and first births than in postponing the initiation of sexual activity. As information about the onset of sexual activity was not ascertained in most Asian countries, the results discussed here for that topic pertain mainly to Africa and Latin America and the Caribbean. Among men, as among women, in the majority of countries the proportion marrying by age 20 decreases as the education level attained increases. Whereas greater educational attainment appears to deter early onset of sexual activity for women, it seems to have the opposite effect among men.

The onset of sexual activity can affect the health of adolescents, as adolescents often do not seek prenatal care for various reasons such as fear of parents' reaction, lack of awareness of the pregnancy or of the availability of prenatal care, or fear of expulsion from school. In the majority of countries, the onset of sexual activity before age 20 and within marriage is more frequent among women and men with no education than among their schooled peers. Premarital sexual activity before age 20 is more common, in a majority of countries, among educated women and men than among their peers with no education.

12.7.8. Education and Fertility

Education plays an important role in improving overall economic and social status, which greatly influences the number and spacing of children desired and eventually attained. Education continues to exert a significant influence on fertility levels, preferences and regulation. At the aggregate level, countries with higher literacy rates and overall educational attainment have lower total fertility rates (TFRs) than countries whose populations have lower education levels. The effect of a country's overall level of education on its TFR exists in both developing and developed countries. Moreover, this effect continues to be significant when other characteristics are controlled for.

Differentials in fertility by educational level also appear in developed countries. Women with higher levels of education desire smaller families. Educational differentials in the mean ideal number of children are greatest in sub-Saharan Africa, where women with no education desire to have 2 children more than women with a secondary or higher education, on average. Wanted fertility rates are substantially lower than actual fertility rates, and this gap also varies across educational subgroups. It is much larger among women with no education or primary education than among women with a secondary or higher education.

12.8. Family Life Education

Family life eduction is an "educational process designed to assist young people in their physical, social, emotional and moral development as they prepare for adulthood, marriage, parenthood, ageing as well as their social relationships in the sociocultural context of the family and society". According to yet another definition family life education has been conceived as an "education for human development, which seeks to ensure that each individual approaching adulthood is equipped with the skills and personal reserves to cope with the challenges of everyday life in society, within acceptable societal structures, and to adapt to change with experience and equilibrium".

Family life education, therefore, is a broader concept than sex or sexuality education. It does not simply deal with the human sexual development and sexual behaviour. It is aimed at enabling individuals to understand and appreciate the institution of family and the family life in proper perspective. It focuses largely on developing among learners the ability to understand themselves and the family and the society in which they live and interact, to think rationally and independently, to clarify the traditional values and their own values and to take informed decisions about their own individual selves and the family life.

In order to facilitate effective integration of family life education in the content and process of school education, it is essential to prepare a conceptual framework which guides the process of integration of its elements in the school curriculum framework, syllabi, textbooks and other components of the teaching-learning process. It is still more important to integrate family life education in the process of teacher preparation, suitably incorporating its elements in the pre-service and in-service teacher education.

Education is considered as one of the most potent instruments of peaceful social change and also a significant means to develop among individuals the ability of self-actualisation and self-realisation. In view of this crucial role education has to respond to the current and emerging needs of the society and aspirations of the people. But by its very nature education continues to be rigid and conservative and quite often tends to defer its response to societal needs. Which is why educational innovations emerge to accelerate the process of its internal transformation, so that education relates itself to the life, needs, aspirations and demands of individuals and reflects the chief concerns of the society. Family life education is one of the educational innovations that are aimed at enabling the existing education system to respond to the emerging needs and requirements.

Family life education, however, has been conceptualised in more than one way, though it has always focused on various dimensions of the institution of family and the life within it. In certain context this concept has been used as a synonym, and also at times as an euphemism of sex education, while in the other it has been designed as an educational intervention to reinforce the process of social learning for better understanding of the institution of family and its crucial role as a basic social institution.

The programme on family life education in some countries was launched when comprehensive efforts were initiated to start the population education during early 1970s as a complementary strategy to help nations attain their demographic goals. Particularly those programmes, which focused on, the teaching of sexual development and sexuality preferred to use the title of family life education. It was thought that since the pace of population growth depended on the Fertility behaviour of individuals, it would be necessary to educate them in sexual development, sexuality, reproduction including conception, pregnancy, pre and post-natal care and child care, so that the educational intervention influenced their attitude and behaviour in respect of reproduction and brought about desirable change in the fertility rate. In some other countries, the need to start such an educational programme was felt in view of the problems faced by the young people because of the lack of authentic knowledge available to the them in respect of physical, physiological, emotional and social development during the process of growing up from childhood to adulthood.

The growing incidence of sexual relationship among adolescents and increasing number of premarital pregnancies coupled with the gradual erosion of the institutions of marriage and family impelled the educational planners to start the process of imparting education in sex and sexuality. Since sex related elements have been considered socio-culturally sensitive, it was preferred to name the educational programme as family life education.

The need to impart education in this sensitive area is felt primarily because the current generation of adolescents is more than a billion strong, and will be the largest generation in history to make the transition from children to adults. But their health needs, and particularly their reproductive health needs, continue to be ignored and neglected. As they stand at the threshold of adulthood, they need authentic knowledge that helps them understand the process of growing up in particular reference to their reproductive health needs, so that they are well equipped to cope with the problems which they confront during the transitional phase. They need both guidance and independence, education as well as opportunities to explore life for themselves in order to attain a level of maturity required to make responsible decisions.

This need is particularly felt in India, because the school curriculum here does not include the crucial elements of reproductive health such as sexual development during the period of adolescence, HIV/AIDS and drug abuse. These are contents on the biological aspects of the reproduction system, but education in these elements cannot be complete by giving simply the biological information. There is a need to focus on physiological, emotional and socio-cultural dimensions of the adolescent reproductive health in a holistic manner. After serious consideration, now a consensus has been reached on the issue of introduction of adolescence education in schools with a view to providing authentic knowledge to students regarding the process of growing up, HIV/AIDS and drug abuse and influencing their attitude, behaviour and value orientation.

There still is a point of view according to which it is not proper to introduce elements relating to sexual development in the school curriculum. People holding such view put forth the following arguments:

(a) Sex and sexuality are intimately private matters which are not to be discussed in public, and that too with young children. In India individuals have been receiving information about these matters indirectly through different sources available in their respective socio-cultural settings. Therefore, there is no need to introduce such an educational programme in Indian schools.

(b If schools start providing knowledge about the sexual development, the young children will be encouraged to experiment with the newly acquired knowledge which is generally exciting. This will promote promiscuity and sexual permissiveness, spoiling the school and social environment. The regular discussion of sex and sexuality which is a treasured sublime instinct of human beings will reduce it to mundane routine affair. The young students will be desensitised and will not be able to appreciate its sublime value in their future lives.

However, these views if considered in the context of the current social reality will not appear to be plausible because of the following reasons:

(a) A number of studies lend support to the fact that adolescents desire and seek authentic knowledge on sexual development, which they experience. But sex being a taboo, no authentic source has been available to them, through which they can get such knowledge. This situation creates anxieties and confusion and generates myths and misconceptions among adolescents about various aspects of their growing up. These myths and misconceptions are carried over to their adulthood, adversely affecting their attitude and behaviour throughout their lives.

(b) Since the average age at marriage is increasing and the age of puberty is advancing, the young people have a longer interval between their sexual maturity and marriage. This situation has increased the possibility of their being engaged in premarital sexual relationships. Studies, conducted in different cultural settings have found the growing incidence of premarital sexual relations among adolescents. It is, therefore considered necessary for the school curriculum to equip adolescents well, so that they manage their sexual development responsibly and develop a healthy attitude towards sex.

(c) The media reports highlight almost regularly the growing incidence of sex crimes in our society. The particular matter of great concern is the problem of sexual abuse and exploitation of young girls and even minors. These situations demand urgent educational intervention, so that young children are made aware of the implications of sexual development in them and the need to respect the inviolability of every person and to safeguard themselves against such inhuman incidents.

(d) The impact of traditional value system that used to influence the sex-related behaviour of individuals has been waning because of certain new trends in social development such as urbanisation with its widespread impact on human life, migration to slums in the cities and the changing lifestyles. There is a need to reinforce those social and cultural values that militate against irresponsible sexual behaviour.

(e) Even when adolescence education is not being imparted, children and adolescents are exposed to sex-related issues, and that too mostly in a crude manner, through other sources like cinema, film magazines and other periodicals, video parlours, commercial advertisements and certain sensuous programmes telecast on domestic and foreign channels of television. Even newspapers are devoting increasing space to sex-related stories. It will, therefore, be better to impart adolescence education to adolescents, so that they may appreciate such exposures in proper perspective.

(f) The AIDS pandemic has added urgency to introduce adolescence education in schools. Although HIV, the virus that leads to AIDS, can be transmitted through blood and from the infected mother to her child, the principal mode of transmission is through sexual relations. The sharing of syringes and needles by drug addicts is also a potential route of HIV transmission. Studies have come out with the finding that adolescents are the greatest victims of HIV infection. Since there is no vaccine or cure available for HIV/AIDS, preventive education is the only means to promote behavioural changes which can prevent HIV infection.

(g) The increasing incidence of smoking and use of tobacco, alcohol and other dangerous drugs by young children is assuming alarming proportion. Young adolescents tend to see the use of these drugs as part of being grown up. It is, therefore, urgently needed to educate them in drug abuse and motivate them against drug addiction.

(h) The apprehensions of adults in respect of introduction of adolescence education in schools have been proved to be misplaced. Studies indicate that education about reproductive and sexual health does not encourage students to experiment with their newly acquired knowledge. Rather, it encourages them to have positive attitude towards sex and inculcate responsible behaviour.

(i) The apprehension of teachers that the teaching of elements of adolescence education will tarnish their "image" and promote indiscipline among students has also been negated by a number of studies. Wherever, teachers are responsive to the needs of adolescent students and provide guidance to them to cope with their problems, the teacher-pupil relation has become better and the school environment has improved.

(j) There has been a significant change in the perception of adult members of the society, particularly parents and teachers, towards the introduction of adolescence education in schools. Although students always felt the need to get eduction in sex related matters, parents and teachers had serious apprehensions till very recently. But now a number of studies conducted in different States have found that parents and teachers overwhelmingly favour the introduction of adolescence eduction in schools.

Moreover, it is pertinent to note that family life eduction has been conceived in a much broader context. It has been felt for quite some time that the family, which is thc basic unit of society has been under strains. Many forces such as industrialisation, rapid demographic and socio-economic changes, widespread migration, urbanisation, poverty, weaking of the institution of marriage, and liberalised code of sexual ethics have influenced the pattern of family formation and family life. These have not only generated considerable changes in family composition and structure but also eroded its significance as a key social institution. The traditional notion of relationships within the family does not reflect the current reality and aspirations.

Family is an agent of social learning is constrained to perform its educational functions. It is also found wanting in the task of preparing its younger members for adulthood. With the changing age structure, care for the aged is increasingly becoming an emerging concern within the family. Education is, therefore, expected to reaniment the family life, help foster family solidarity, enable family members to cope with the changing demands of different stages of family life and to ensure wholesome relationships among family members.

12.8.1. Teaching Methods

The traditional teaching methods may not be effective for imparting family life education, primarily because of the sensitive nature of its contents and its focus on influencing the affective domain of learners. Therefore, non-conventional methods of teaching like values clarification, enquiry method, problem solving method and other interactive mode of teaching may be adopted. Students need to be increasingly involved in co-curricular activities focused on the critical concerns of family life education.

12.8.2. Evaluation

Evaluation is an integral part of the institutionalisation of family life education in the existing education system. All aspects of evaluation—context evaluation, process evaluation, product evaluation—are significant. The context evaluation may be conducted to identify the relevant concerns of family life education in different cultural settings and content analysing the existing syllabi and textbooks to identify gaps as well as suitable entry points for integration of its elements. Evaluation needs to be made an integral part of material development, training, teaching-leaming and organising various educational activities. Impact studies, though, difficult and challenging, are necessary not only to assess the attainment of objectives but also to identify gaps in instructional strategies and to take corrective measures.

12.9. Conclusion

Education is a fundamental human right, as clearly articulated in article 26 of the Universal Declaration of Human Rights. Beyond its intrinsic human value, "education is also an indispensable means of unlocking and protecting other human rights by providing the scaffold required to secure good health, liberty, security, economic well-being and participation in social and political activity". Education-especially good quality education-has a positive impact not only on a country's economic development, but also on better health, lower fertility and maternal mortality, less risk of exposure to HIV/AIDS and greater life expectancy. It has a "powerful impact in addressing social and economic barriers within a society and is central to realising human freedoms."

Although education has an impact on human and economic development, its own development can be impeded by the influence of a range of demographic, economic, social, cultural and political factors. Population growth, for instance, can affect the demand for and supply of education in such a way as it can facilitate or hinder efforts to achieve universal primary education (UPE), especially when it is rapid and within a context of resource constraints.

References

Jayasuriya, J.E., *Curriculum innovation through population education,* Colombo: Associated Educational Publishers, 1978.

Kline, David and David Harman ed., *Issues in population education*, Lexington, Mass: Lexington Books, 1976.

Sikes, O.J., "Reconceptualization of population education"*, Technical Paper,* Number 2, UNFPA, New York: 1993.

Unesco, Regional Office for Education in Asia and the Pacific, "Problems and strategies for curriculum development in population education", *A paper presented to the Group Training course in Population Education*, Bangkok: 14 July to 15 August 1975.

........., "Population education: innovative structures and approaches", *Report of a Regional Workshop*, New Delhi, 23-29 October 1979.

........., "Future directions of population education", *Report of a Regional Consultative Seminar*, Manila, 14-21 August 1978.

CHAPTER 13

Population Control Measures in India and China

13.1. Introduction

Today no problem is made urgently important to the well being of mankind than the limitation of population growth. It is a problem, the effects of which are world-wide demanding the attention of all nations- east and west large and small, developed and developing. Too rapid population growth hinders a nations ability to progress and to satisfy the growing demands of its people for a better life.

Population growth around the world effect all people through its impact on national economies, the environment, safety and health and the habitability of the world children will inherit. Two points on the interaction of population dynamics and human well being stand out. Population growth may have different impacts depending on when, where and how it occur through decreases/increases, death rate birth rate or immigration. The impact depend not just on the rate of growth but on the size and age structure of the existing population, the resources as water and crop land and the adaptability of the societies in which population growth is occurring. The second point is that population growth influences many areas of human affairs. The issue is not merely food security or health or environmental quality or economic growth, but all this and more because high population growth rate cause of poverty, low standard of living, malnutrition, ill health, environmental degradation and a wide other social problems. If we discuss about the population cycle too rapid, a population growth rate yields negative economic consequences and psychological problems associated with the conditions of under employment. Population growth retards the prospects of a better life because problem of population is not simply of numbers. It also evolves the quality of life and material well being. The population size also intensify the problem of under development.

In our lifetimes humanity has become a force on the planet. The reasons for this are complex and linked to changes not only in human population but in technologies consumption patterns, unequal distribution, choices made by people business and governments. The consequences of rapid population growth can be vivid in light of the carrying capacity of the earth but also and more importantly in relation to human capacities to improve welfare and reduce poverty. Rapid population growth raises concern at three levels of human experience: global resource sufficiency, national and local institutional capacity and individual family welfare.

The growth of world population and production combined with unsustainable consumption patterns places increasingly severe strain on the life supporting capabilities on our earth. These interactive processes effect the use of land, water, air, energy and other resources. Rapid growth and the high dependency ratio lead to another phenomenon called the "Hidden Momentum of Population Growth" means the population has the tendency to grow rapidly even after achieving the low fertility rates. The basic reason for this hidden momentum is that high birth rates cannot be brought down overnight.

The social, economic and institutional forces that has influenced the fertility rates over the course of centuries increase in population, within the last two centuries. The rural as well as the urban poor have been hardest hit. The available resources do not suffice for number of people we have. If the population growth is not effectively and immediately checked, the population bomb may prove to be more dangerous than the atom bomb.

13.1.1. Youth Population

Today 1.05 billion is the biggest even generation of young, people between 15 to 24 years. This age group is rapidly expanding in many countries specially in the third world, population is very youthful particularly where children under the age of 15 constitute almost 40% of the population, as compared with the 21% of the developed world. In Sweden and U.K the work force constitute almost 65% of the total population while only 18-19% are youth dependence is almost 50-50. The more rapid the population growth rate, the greater will be the proportion of the dependent children, they have special needs for health care and education, including the most important area of sexual and reproductive health.

The least developed countries are early in the transition from high to low birth and death rates, their population are concentrated in the younger ages. In time as fertility and mortality fall, their population structure will more closely resemble between now and 2010. Seven hundred million young people will enter the labour force in developing countries which is more than the entire labour force of the developed countries in 1990. In many developing countries the next 10 years will be the critical years.

13.1.2. Ageing Population

Better medical care is preserving life through low death rate resulting more people living longer. In the more developed regions, the proportion of the population above 65 years has increased from 7.9 in 1950 to 13.5 percent today and is expected to reach 24.7 percent by the year 2050. The most rapidly aging countries will exceed 40% of their population at older ages. In some countries, population above the age of 85 years will more than double in the same period. Currently about 77% of the increase in older population is taking place in developing region. Over the first decade of the next century, there will thus be a gradual demographic shift towards an older population in all countries.

13.1.3. Poverty and Food

The earth's land total area is 13 billion sq. Hectares. The food of the future will be produced on today's farmland. Only 11% of the world's land surface i.e. 1.44 billion hectars is now farmed. There is little additional land that can be converted to crop land and farm sustainability. Many countries will be unable to pay for the food their people need, raises the risk of dependence on food aid. Industrialisation and urbanisation has led to environment disorder. Urban population is growing faster. The average growth rate for cities in developing countries is 3.5 percent a year compared to 1.9 percent for these countries as a whole. People move to cities to improve their economic and educational standards and quality of life but unskilled migrated labour is bound to live in slums at low standard and below poverty line.

Population growth cannot continue indefinitely on a finite planet. Policy initiatives that result in lower birth rates bring societies closer to the day when population growth no longer act as a complicating force in human life. Slowing population growth brings societies closer to population stability a prerequisite for true natural resource sustainability for the economic and social under pinnings of human well being.

Actions are recommended to help couples and individuals meet their reproductive goals to prevent unwanted pregnancies and reduce the incidence of high risk pregnancies and morbidity and mortality, to make quality services affordable, acceptable and accessable to all who need and want them, to improve the quality of advice, information education communication, counselling and services, to increase the participation and sharing of responsibility of men in the actual practice of Family Planning.

13.1.4. Population Policy in Asia-Pacific Region

Many countries in Asia have formulated effective population policies and successfully implemented family planning, maternal and child health programmes in order to achieve their demographic goals like lowering fertility rates, raising the expectation of life at birth, reducing infant mortality rates and thereby slowing population growth rates.

The Population growth rate among Asian countries divide the regions into two groups: one group of countries with high population growth rates exceeding 2.0% per year and the other with moderate or low growth rates of 1.4% or lower. Population policy and programmes are different in these two groups. Where fertility is high the main demographic goals is to reduce responsible demographic factors as birth rate, death rate, infant mortality rate, growth rate, in addition to creating employment opportunities for the rapidly expanding working group population and also concentrating more on improving the quality of life of their population.

The alarming population growth is creating increased pressure on the infrastructure, economy, environment, availability of health services and nutrition. Rapid population growth affects various socio-economic aspects and the quality of life. Despite the rapid population growth, certain development indicators show heartening achievements; advances in health care and overall socio-economic progress is reflected in the demographic transition that has occurred over the last few decades.

There are number of factors that contribute to population growth. Some of the reasons for high fertility are, low age at marriage, illiteracy and unmet need for contraceptives. Other factors such as poor health care services also have impact on population growth. If people already have big family size before accepting FP, this does not lead to a reduction in population growth. In Indian context, it has been observed that a poor status of women and low female literacy also contribute to high fertility. Cultural factors such as son preference, the desire for old age security and perceiving children as assets have also contributed to rapid population growth in India.

13.1.5. Density of Population

Density of Population is the number of persons per sq. km. and is arrived at dividing the number of persons by the total area of a region/country. In the last more than 70 years since 1921, the density of population has been rising and particularly since 1951, there has been a rapid rise. The change in the density has varied from state to state. In some states it has increased much in others comparatively less. Reasons being India is primarily an agricultural country and factors like climate, rain fall, irrigation facilities etc. have a great influence on density of population. Another factor has been the development of industries in different states/regions. Besides, there are other factors that have influenced density in different places such as religions and historical importance of places, availability of educational facilities and the existence of administrative offices etc.

13.1.6. Distribution of Population in Rural-urban Areas

Another striking feature of India's population which has persisted for long is the predominance of rural population. As per 1991 census as much as 74.3 % of the population lives in rural areas. The urbanites constitute 25.7 percent, as against 78 percent in England, 77 percent in Sweden and 74 percent in U.S.A. Over time since 1951 there has been a change in the ratio of rural urban population but of only some significance. The Indian economy can be described as a rural economy, as against western economies, often designated as industrial/urban economies.

13.2. Evolving Population Policies in India and China

The world's two population billionaires, India and China, have established national policies to address population growth, though they differ greatly in their details and implementation. Although both countries have substantial regional variation, China's policy has been strictly enforced nationwide and more effective than India's in dramatically reducing fertility and slowing population growth. But China's "success" has also met with international criticism because it limits women's freedom to bear children. The experiences of these large countries affect and respond to global discussions about population and individual rights.

The State Family Planning Commission introduced the reforms gradually by selecting pilot counties where family planning services would offer a range of contraceptive method choices, reproductive health care, and counseling. Although local officials still set family planning targets, the concept of "informed choice" has gained acceptance, and an estimated 25 percent of all counties in China have reformed their family planning services to some degree.

Though the policy is credited with reducing the total fertility rate from 5.8 in 1970 to less than 2 in 2000 and averting an estimated 300 million births, the government is increasingly faced with the negative side of the changes it brought about. There are fewer children and grandchildren to care for the growing number of elderly people, and limits on childbearing have exacerbated couples' traditional preference for sons, leading to sex-selective abortions, female infanticide, and a deficit of girls in the country. Increasing individual freedoms, market-oriented economic reforms, and greater openness to the global community all point toward a more relaxed approach to family planning. But the government's public stance indicates a continued interest in controlling population growth.

13.3. Population Policies in India

Each year India adds more people to the world's population than any other country. In 1997, there were almost as many babies born in India (about 25 million) as in all of Sub-Saharan Africa and more than in China (21 million). India's total fertility rate is declining but the continued increase in the number of women of reproductive age suggests continued high numbers of births. India's States vary widely with respect to fertility, mortality, and contraceptive use. In general, there is a north/south gradient-most western and southern States have lower mortality, lower fertility, and higher contraceptive use. In the north, Uttar Pradesh, the most populous State, has high mortality, low contraceptive use, and the highest fertility.

In the 1950s, India launched the world's first state-sponsored family planning programme to slow population growth. From the early 1960s to the mid-1990s, government-determined targets for contraceptive use dominated the management of the programme. Between 1975 and 1977, Prime Minister Indira Gandhi's government promoted male sterilisation campaigns that sometimes led to coercion. Public outrage about the reported abuses contributed to the downfall of Gandhi's government and created a backlash against family planning programmes that took years to overcome.

In the 1980s and 1990s, the government continued supporting the national family planning programme with centrally mandated targets for contraceptive use. Although acceptance of family planning was voluntary, the apparent zeal to achieve the targets again met with growing criticism. Critics argued that the overemphasis on reaching annual targets led health workers to worry about meeting numerical goals rather than meeting the needs of the women they served. In 1996, the Indian government made a major policy shift by announcing the 'Target-Free Approach' to family planning, eliminating all centrally mandated targets for contraceptive acceptance. Targets remained for planning purposes at the local and state levels, but health workers and administrators were no longer to be reprimanded for not meeting them.

The new approach, called the reproductive and child health approach, was being implemented unevenly throughout the vast and populous states of India. This is not surprising given the decentralised government and the tremendous economic and social diversity in the country. The 2000 national population policy calls for reducing the average family size from 3.2 in 1999 to 2.1 children per woman by 2010, which would require a rapid decline in birth rates. To achieve this goal, the policy calls for meeting the needs for family planning and other health care and for integrated reproductive and child health care services. In India's largest and poorest states, expanding and improving these services will require substantially greater resources and human capacity.

Regarding intervention in population control and the qualitative composition of India's population-- during the Emergency the Population Policy furthered the inimical rift between India's Hindus and Muslims by legitimising traditional enmities and increasing concerns about protecting 'vote banks' in the Government. To ebb the possibility of violent uprisings or any more divisions in the wake of the Bangladesh War, the government assured via policy action that parliamentary seats and the allocation of central funds would not be affected by a state's population control performance.

India has illustrated that in theory, political intervention in family planning and fertility behaviour can be brought into harmony with human rights if certain conditions are in place. In India, this would include: 1) a fully functioning democracy, because the Emergency illustrated that political intervention in fertility behavior cannot be successfully pursued when legislative and executive frameworks are impaired, and 2) that political intervention and the methods by which it is implemented be focused on family planning and health rather than population control. The one caveat is that even if circumstances are ideal, deeply engrained traditional values pose a challenge to rights based political interventions into family planning. It is conceivable that if the population policy transition is to last in India, whereas politics is harmonised with human rights, then policies will have to utilise lessons learned from events that occurred during the Emergency and take a multidisciplinary approach that acknowledges the large extent to which population policies have an effect on the health, personal convictions, and entitled freedoms of citizens.

13.3.1. Population Size and Growth

India will most likely surpass China in population size by about the middle of the next century. India's population is currently growing at a rate (1.7 percent annually) about 70 percent higher than that of China and will continue growing faster than China for many years in the future. Currently, India has a young population which will grow somewhat older largely as a result of the fertility decline which is already underway. Between now and 2020, both the working age population and the number of women in childbearing ages will grow more rapidly and will become larger proportions of the total population than now.

13.3.2. Mortality and HIV/AIDS

India, like other developing countries, has achieved substantial improvements in mortality. Since independence, life expectancy has roughly doubled from about 32-33 years to 62 years in 1997. The infant mortality rate (IMR) has been reduced from 200-225 infant deaths per 1,000 births to 66. India has a lower IMR than its immediate neighbours-Pakistan and Bangladesh-but a much higher rate than China, Sri Lanka, and various other South East Asian countries.

Inadequate antenatal care and delivery services, low levels of immunisation among children, and a substantial proportion of highrisk births are some of the reasons for the relatively high mortality of infants and children in India. Future improvements in mortality may be slowed or even stalled by the HIV/AIDS epidemic in India. While HIV was introduced into India at a later date than much of the rest of the world, the epidemic is extensive, with rapid growth in some geographic areas. Studies of high-risk populations (commercial sex workers, intravenous drug users, and sexually transmitted disease patients) show high and rapidly rising rates of HIV infection, exceeding 50 percent in some areas of the country. The virus also is spreading in the general population.

13.3.3. Fertility

Fertility in India has declined substantially, from a total fertility rate (TFR) of 5.7 children per woman in the mid-1960's to 3.3 children in 1997. Since the mid-1960's, India has covered two-thirds of the distance to the replacement fertility of just over two births per woman. Fertility varies widely among States; it is significantly below the national average in the southern and western States and higher in the others.

13.3.4. Contraceptive Prevalence

The national family planning programme, which was established in 1952, has played an important role in India's fertility decline. When the programme began, there was little awareness or use of modern birth control methods. Four decades later, the 1992-93 National Family Health Survey (NFHS) found nearly universal knowledge of family planning, with 96 percent of married women ages 13 to 49 years having heard of at least one modern method, and almost 41 percent, or almost 70 million women, using contraception.

Eighty-nine percent of married women who practiced family planning in India relied upon modern contraceptive methods. Female sterilisation, the method, which is strongly promoted by India's family planning programme, was by far the most widely used method. Nearly 67 percent of married women who were using contraception, or 47 million women, had been sterilised compared with an average of only 30 percent for the entire world. Education, religion, place and

State of residence are among the factors that strongly correlate with contraceptive use in India. Nearly half of the married women with some primary schooling use contraception compared with one third of illiterate women. Differentials by religion are also strong.

Among the major States, contraceptive use ranges from more than 63 percent of married women using contraceptives in Kerala to less than 20 percent in Uttar Pradesh.

13.3.5. Fertility Preference and Family Planning

A large majority of married women in India (77 percent) prefer to regulate their fertility. However, the survey found an incongruence between women's desire and actual practice to regulate their fertility. If there were no unwanted births in India, its TFR would be lower by nearly three quarters of a child. For Uttar Pradesh, avoidance of unwanted births could reduce the TFR by at least one child. A substantial portion of the total demand for family planning services remains unsatisfied.

Unmet need for spacing is a substantial portion of the total unmet need for family planning-most of the unmet need among younger women is for spacing. This suggests that more attention should be given to methods other than sterilisation, such as condom, the pill, and IUD. Further, fully meeting today's unmet need for family planning, that is, providing services to an additional 35 million women, will require substantial additional resources.

Further direct evidence supporting the view that the family welfare programme should pay greater attention to temporary methods of family planning-the pill, IUD, condom, and injections-comes from the responses of intended users in the future which show that the potential demand for these methods is substantial. According to the NFHS, nearly 31 percent of noncontracepting married women in India who intend to use family planning in the future indicate preference for temporary methods.

13.3.6. Literacy

Literacy and education, especially of females, affect fertility through greater access and practice of contraception and desire for smaller family size. Literacy in India has improved steadily. Although female literacy in India has improved at a faster rate than that of men, in 1995 women continued to have a much lower rate (38 percent) than men (66 percent). Efforts continue to improve schooling and literacy, especially for girls and women. Many States have begun "total literacy campaigns" to eliminate illiteracy among the disadvantaged population ages 15 to 34.

13.4. Family Welfare Programme in India

India was the first country in the world to have an official family planning programme. The National Family Planning Programme was launched in India in 1951-52 with the objectives of reducing the birth rate to the extent necessary to stabilise the population at a level consistent with the requirement of national economy. India had a model population policy, which aims to provide family planning services within a broader context of maternal and child health care, emphasising voluntarism and informed choice among contraceptive methods and community participation. Initially the programme started mainly for controlling population but it has evolved over the decades in the light of experience gained within the country and in the light of international experience.

13.4.1. Origin of Family Planning Programne

Prof. R.D. Karve opened the country's first Family Planning clinic in Pune in the year 1923. After that a society for the study and promotion of family hygiene was formed in Bombay in the year 1935. In the year 1938, Subash Chander Bose, President of Indian National Congress advocated a restriction of India's population size. He set up the National Planning Committee under the Chairmanship of Pt. Jawaharlal Nehru. All India women's conference began advocating the adoption of voluntary birth control. Under the leadership of Smt. Dhanvanti Rama Rao Family Planning Association of India (FPAI) was established in 1949. After independence, Pt. Jawaharlal Nehru appointed a sub committee chaired by Dr. Radha Kamal Mukherjee to look into various aspects of India's population problems. The Committee recommended the establishment of birth control clinics.

The Planning Commission set up in March 1950 accepted the recommendations of the committee on population growth and Family Planning. The final draft was released in December 1952, highlighting the urgency of the Family Planning and Population control. The commission created two committees, one to address policy and approach and other to address research and programmes on population and Family Planning.

In the second five year plan Family Planning and other supporting programmes for raising the standard of the health and the people throughout rural India under the umbrella of a community development programme were enviseged. In 1959, our Government accepted sterilisation as one of the recognised methods of family size limitation.

The number of family planning clinics was proposed to increase from 147 to 8200 during 1952-1966 period. Through clinics the Family Planning programmes broadened by intensified sterilisation programme, the use of condoms and IUD were promoted. The fourth plan proposed recruitment of more female doctors, involving private medical practitioners and implementing the programme on a co-ordinated basis by involving other ministries. The medical termination of pregnancy act was passed by the Indian Parliament and come into force from April 1972.

13.4.2. National Population Policy - 1976

Dr. Karan Singh then Minister of Health and Family Welfare submitted National Population Policy on 16th April 1976. In the document it has been mentioned that on 1st January 1976, India has crossed the six hundred million mark. As per policy, our real problems are poverty, illiteracy, ignorance and superstition which should be eliminated only then the nation will be able to move forward to its desired ideals. He further stated that simply waiting for education and economic development to bring down the fertility is not a practical solution.

In nutshell it can be concluded that the success of Family Welfare programme is dependent on i) adequate availability of resources ii) effective public support by opinion leaders and citizens iii) effectiveness of the health system and efficient services for delivery iv) effective collateral programmes for educating literacy for women, empowerment of women and fast economic improvement.

13.4.3. Launching of Reproductive Child Health Programme

For over 44 years, the FP programmes in India has popularised the small family norm. People have not responded enthusiastically to this because they were not sure if children born to them would survive and be healthy. Government launched several successful initiatives that reduced child mortality such as universal immunisation programme (UIP) child survival and safe motherhood (CSSM) programme and the reproductive and child health programme. The Reproductive and Child Health Programme was undertaken on 15th October 1997 drawing its mandate from the programme of action of the international conference on population and development in 1994. Under the RCH programme, a comprehensive package of services for FP, maternal and child health and management of reproductive track infection (RTI) including Sexually transmitted diseases (STD) will be implemented. Inputs will be provided to improve the services to bridge the gap between services provided and unmet needs. In addition, efforts will be made to improve the availability of the services from bottom to top. In a nutshell RCH will cover the services offered under the CSSM and FW programme as well as two new interventions namely management of RTI and adolescent reproductive health. This programme will cover mothers and children adolescents, parents and eligible couples.

13.4.4. Programme Strategy

There is a wide gap between awareness about health and family welfare and acceptance of services. Although services are available but people do not know about them. Even when awareness is high, attitudes do not necessarily change or new behaviour practiced. For the purpose IEC activities will be planned at the Primary Health Centre level after identifying service and communication needs in the area. Through this, IEC will promote awareness regarding increasing age of marriage, nutrition, pregnancy, feeding of calustrum practices, birth spacing, good sanitary practices.

Finally, it can be concluded that the responsibility of making the RCH programme a success lies in the hands of health managers, workers and the people. It is expected that the programme will have wide acceptance and ownership not only because it will be developed with people's inputs but also because it will raise the standards of quality. Quality will determine the effectiveness of this programme in relation to reducing fertility, which will lead to population control of the nation.

13.4.5. Impact and Achievements of Family Welfare Programme

National Family Welfare programmes has been successful in generating universal awareness of FP. A vast infrastructure comprising of health workers and health facilities has been established to provide FP information and services to couples. As a result of FP measures about 210 million births have been averted up to 1997. There has been a decline in the total fertility rate or the average number of children born to a woman. The TFR has dropped from 6 at the time of independence to about 3 in 1994, the crude birth rate has also gone down from 41.7 in 1951 to 28 per thousand in 1998. The couple protection rate in 1971 was 10.4%, which increased to 46.5% in 1996.

While linkages among population, education and development have long been recognised, the priority accorded to these relationships has varied. In the decades following the Second World War, education was a high priority for many Governments, and educational systems underwent a rapid expansion. By the 1980s, however, faltering

economies, debt-service burdens and structural adjustment programmes had led some countries to reduce the provision of public services, including education. It was generally in the poor countries that education budgets suffered the most, and enrolment ratios declined in some cases, especially in sub-Saharan Africa. At the same time, the understanding of the process of development was also changing in ways that accorded education a more prominent role. In the decades immediately after the Second World War, professional economists concerned with development focused mainly on growth in output (gross national product (GNP)) as the indicator of progress, and especially on industrialisation and trade issues as determinants of growth. While there was surely a consensus that a high level of economic development could not be achieved

with a largely illiterate populace, formal economic models generally paid little attention to "human capital" as a determinant of economic growth; however, this gradually changed. A growing number of economists found evidence that human capital - particularly education and health - had important economic benefits society-wide. Beyond this, the whole concept of development evolved, shifting from a narrow vision to one that encompassed the broader relationships among socio-economic development, poverty and the environment. There was also a greater recognition that, over and above its strictly economic effects, education helped foster progress towards other goals such as better health and longer life, personal development, participation in civil society and access to a wider range of opportunities.

Despite demographic pressures in many developing countries during the period 1960-1980, school enrolment grew at an unprecedented pace, enrolment ratios rose and class sizes generally declined. Schultz found that, controlling for per capita income, enrolment ratios were no lower in countries where the proportion of population of school age was high. Effects of the rapid growth in the school-age population on school quality are less clear. The cross-national evidence suggests that school expenditures generally do not increase in response to an increase in the size of the school-aged cohort, in other words, spending per school-age child tends to be lower where the "demographic burden" is greater.

13.5. Population Policies in China

China has been the world's most populous country for centuries and today makes up one-fifth of the world's population. It is no surprise that China's huge population, tumultuous demographic history, and possible future have attracted the world's attention. The country's growing economic strength, combined with its demographic might, ensures it will stay in the limelight for a long time to come.

The country has undergone enormous social, economic, and political changes over the past 50 years, but many of the issues that Chinese society faces today are also closely connected to past demographic change. Because of the rapid and extensive fertility declines in China in the past 30 years, the country's rate of population growth has slowed considerably. The country's population of 1.3 billion in the early 2000s is projected to grow by another 100 million by 2050. India-with its higher fertility levels-is forecast to move ahead of China in total population size by 2035.

China covers about the same geographic area as the United States, although its population is nearly five times greater. In addition, because of rugged mountains in the west and vast desert areas in central China, the population is concentrated within a surprisingly small area. Rapid population growth during the 20th century helped shaped China's society in myriad ways as China concurrently struggled with the breakdown of its dynastic structure, world wars, civil wars, and the founding of a new nation. The 20th century was a time of momentous changes for the Chinese people, and demographic change was very much a part of their social and political transformation.

13.5.1. Political Change

China's population has undergone massive change since the founding of the People's Republic of China (PRC) in 1949. When the Chinese Communists formed the new government, there were roughly one-half billion Chinese. Millions of peasants lived in abject poverty, subject to unstable political conditions. Chinese had endured a civil war, war with Japan, serious flooding, famine, and social and political turmoil. China's new leaders were determined to reduce poverty and stabilise the political situation.

13.5.2. Mortality Decline

China's mortality has declined dramatically over the past 50 years, especially in the early years of the People's Republic. The official death rate in 1953 was 14 deaths per 1,000 people, but it was probably much higher because mortality was chronically underestimated.

13.5.3. The Great Leap Forward

In 1958, the Chinese government launched the Great Leap Forward, a massive effort to rapidly increase agricultural and industrial production. The programme was a colossal failure and, ironically, caused one of the largest famines in human history. Demographers and others who pieced together the available information have estimated that more than 30 million people died between 1958 and 1961 as a result of the Great Leap Forward. Infants were especially vulnerable. Infant mortality rates spiked in 1958 and again in 1961. Adult mortality surged in 1960. As the country recovered, mortality levels declined and life expectancy at birth increased-from 35 years in 1949 to 72 years in 2001.

13.5.4. Expanding Health Care

While much of the mortality decline can be attributed to rising living standards, the extensive public health system underwritten and organised by the government also helped reduce illness and death. "Barefoot doctors," peasants who received rudimentary medical training, brought preventive and basic health care to millions of rural Chinese. Immunisation programmes were widespread; by 1990, 98 percent of infants had been immunised against polio and measles. The PRC's socialist government also financed all health services and made health care affordable for all citizens.

13.5.5. Health Care After Reforms

The economic reforms of the 1980s that pushed China toward a market economy altered China's health care system in ways that may widen mortality gaps among population groups. In the PRC's early years, universal access to health care was a top priority. But the shift toward a market-oriented system since the early 1980s has meant the demise of guaranteed access to health care. Poor people may not be able to pay for health care, and rural residents may not have access to health services, making those groups particularly vulnerable. Regional, gender, and other differences in mortality are increasingly visible.

13.5.6. Health and Mortality

Mortality rates are notably higher in rural than in urban areas, among the poor, ethnic minorities, and among women. Some of these groups have seen increases in mortality in recent years.

13.5.7. Rural-Urban Gap

The rural-urban mortality gap is persistent and growing. Rural health problems and higher mortality are tied to lower living standards and inadequate health services. Malnutrition, preventable and treatable diseases of infancy, and serious gynecological conditions are much more common in rural areas than in cities. In general, an area's mortality rate is closely related to its per capita net income and its per capita industrial and agricultural output - and many rural areas rank poorly on these indicators. The differences in the leading causes of death reflect the gaps in living standards. In the 1990s, respiratory diseases were the leading cause of death in rural areas; these often preventable deaths accounted for more than 25 percent of all rural deaths, compared with 16 percent of all urban deaths. In contrast, cerebrovascular diseases-associated with older adults-are the leading cause of death in urban areas.

13.5.8. Gender and Life Expectancy

Lower fertility and wider access to modern contraception have helped women avoid frequent and risky pregnancies and reduced maternal mortality. But female advantage also reflects the increased health risks men now face from greater occupational hazards and decades of increasing tobacco use. Mortality among the elderly has not declined significantly since the mid-1970s. The chronic diseases prevalent among this group are not easily addressed through basic health improvements, and China does not have the extensive resources needed to deal with such diseases. Young adults have also seen little change in mortality rates over the past 20 years, primarily because their mortality was already fairly low.

13.5.9. Infant and Child Mortality

Infant mortality has also declined dramatically, although the actual magnitude of the decline is uncertain because data on infant deaths are incomplete. The most reliable estimates suggest that the infant mortality rate fell from 139 infant deaths per 1,000 live births in 1954 to about 41 infant deaths per 1,000 in the late 1990s. China continues to combat infectious diseases likely to strike children, and wide-reaching immunisation programmes have reduced the prevalence of encephalitis, meningitis, and hepatitis.

In addition, improvements in water quality, especially in rural areas, have helped prevent intestinal diseases such as diarrhea, typhoid, and cholera that particularly affect children. Infant mortality has declined most sharply among rural and illiterate citizens, and it has also fallen more sharply among boys than girls. The steep declines in infant and child mortality in China resemble patterns observed in other developing countries, as preventable and curable diseases become less important than genetic problems and it associated with childbirth.

Social and economic changes have played an important indirect role in reducing infant and child mortality and illness. Infant and child-care centers are much more widely available now, especially in cities, which may give workingwomen access to better childcare. The birth-planning programme also contributed to lower child mortality by encouraging women to wait longer between pregnancies, thus easing health demands on women and giving parents more time to care for each child. Parents with fewer children generally have more resources-including time, food, and money-to devote to each child. Social and economic changes can also put children at greater risk of social and physical problems. With more women working full time mothers may spend less time with their young children than mothers did in the past, and grandparents may have less time to care for their grandchildren.

13.5.10. Birth Planning Policies

China's fertility decline has been supported by some of the world's most restrictive national birth planning policies. The most strict and controversial policy began in 1979, but the Chinese government was involved in birth planning beginning in the 1950s. In the early days of the PRC, the government argued that China needed a large population to bolster its political strength and provide labour for economic development. In the mid-1950s, fears that excessive growth would hinder economic development and a desire to improve maternal and child health led the government to reverse its position and look for ways to control population growth.

The first birth planning campaign, in the 1950s, extolled fertility control in the name of maternal and infant well-being. During the second family planning campaign, which began in 1962 and lasted until the start of the Cultural Revolution in 1966, the government sought to lower fertility, especially in rural areas. Much of this campaign was educational; it attempted to teach rural families about the benefits of smaller families.

The government encouraged later marriage, longer intervals between births, and smaller families. To this end, the government tried to increase access to contraceptives and abortions. Fertility in some urban areas declined remarkably during this period, but the campaign had little effect on most rural areas, which were ill-equipped to provide family planning services to large numbers of women. By the end of the 1960s, few people in the central government doubted the importance of birth planning and population control for economic development. China began to produce its own contraceptive devices and, by 1972, was considered self-sufficient.

The third population campaign-wan, xi, shao ("later, longer, fewer")-also emphasised later marriage, longer intervals between births, and fewer births. It began in 1971 and continued until the end of the decade. The campaign had far wider geographic and demographic impacts than any earlier efforts. Rural health services were expanded and contraceptive and abortion services were made available throughout most of the country. The campaign was the first to establish national and provincial level targets for births and-at least in principle-was the basis for targets at local levels. At the start of the campaign, couples were discouraged from having more than two children; by the end of the campaign, in the late 1970s, couples were encouraged to stop after one child.

By the end of the 1970s, the government had begun to believe that population control would require extreme measures. This conviction came partly from a new understanding of the demographic consequences of large birth cohorts; such cohorts would have an echo effect for generations to come, fueling population growth even if fertility fell immediately to replacement level. In addition, the new regime of Deng Xiaoping staked its legitimacy on achieving prosperity by the end of the 20th century-a goal that could be derailed by excessive population growth. "Having seen rampant population growth eat up economic gains in the past, China's leaders were convinced that their economic project would fail if it could not staunch the growth of the population." Rural areas were of particular concern because they accounted for more than 75 percent of all population growth.

These concerns frame the backdrop of China's notorious one-child campaign, launched in 1979. The campaign initially required that all couples have no more than one child and that couples apply for official approval before conceiving a child. Compliance was encouraged through a system of rewards and punishments. Couples who stopped after one child might get preference in educational opportunities, health care, housing, and job assignments. Couples bearing an "out-of-quota" child might be fined or lose access to education or other privileges granted the rest of the populace.

Birth planning policies have changed significantly since the start of the one-child campaign. The campaign has gone through four distinct phases. In the first phase, the government maintained ambitious goals and employed particularly harsh methods to enforce the birth planning policy throughout the country. Rules of contraceptive use were strictly enforced. Incentives and penalties encouraged women to undergo sterilisation after two births. After several years, the government relaxed some of its policies, and ushered in the campaign's second phase.

The government sought to make the policy more realistic and easier for local cadres to enforce, while still meeting the 1.2 billion total population goal for 2000. One of the most significant shifts was in response to strong resistance to the one-child limit among China's peasants. The government sought to "open a small hole to close a large one" by allowing families in rural areas to have a second child if the local quotas could still be met. Officials hoped that this concession would mollify some of the overall resistance to the policy and allow the policy to succeed even in those areas where peasant families had a strong desire for more than one child. In addition, by 1985 the central government had quietly changed its population goal from "no more" than 1.2 billion in 2000 to "about" 1.2 billion.

At the end of the 1980s, new data indicated that fertility levels were still unacceptably high, and the policies were again tightened. Under this third phase of China's birth policies, local efforts were strengthened through changes in incentives and disincentives, the organisation of family planning work, and the allocation of resources. By 1993, the director of the State Family Planning Commission declared that these new efforts and methods had succeeded and that fertility was again under control. The fourth stage, initiated in 2000 and 2001, marked another shift away from the more stringent measures. While adhering to previous birth planning goals, the new approach authorises more client-centered services. Chinese citizens are still obliged to strictly limit the number of children they bear.

13.5.11. Criticism and Resistance

The birth planning programme has come under fire from critics within and outside of China on the grounds that the programme disregards human rights, and many Chinese citizens continue to resist the policy. Most critics acknowledge that fertility control is necessary to limit population growth, but insist that such control does not have to be as harsh as it is now. Even the Chinese government admits there have been instances and periods of coercion surrounding women's reproductive decisions. But some also stress that the Chinese view of population control differs from the Western perspective, and should not be judged by Western values.

In many countries, programmes are called "family planning" programmes to emphasise the dissemination of information and technology that allows couples or individuals to plan how many children to have and when to have them. China's programme is more accurately named a "birth planning" or "population planning" programme, reflecting the theory that human procreation and material production must be in balance in a socialist society. Birth planning is thus considered a societal effort rather than an individualised process.

By the late 1970s, Chinese leaders saw population control as a central part of economic growth planning. The state's role in birth planning is not viewed as an invasion into private matters because private and public interests are considered inseparable. Some Chinese citizens, especially in rural areas, have chafed under the restrictions on the number of births they can have. Villagers often see children (especially sons) as vital to the very meaning of family and necessary for economic and cultural survival. Most rural Chinese accept the state's jurisdiction in their private lives if it is necessary to meet the needs of all citizens, but resist having their own behaviour restricted.

Despite strong disagreement with state policy and birth restrictions, citizens have not openly resisted them. One deterrent to organised resistance may be a feeling that citizens should not speak out against state policy, but the lack of collective action may also reflect the widespread acceptance of state birth planning in China. At the same time, women and their families find ways to circumvent the birth control policies at the individual and family level by hiding their children from authorities, moving to areas where they are unknown to have their children, hiding female infants so that parents can try to have a male child, or surreptitiously removing or not using required contraceptives. The programme's success in the face of ongoing resistance suggests the existence of considerable tensions within China regarding birth planning restrictions.

13.5.12. Fertility Levels

Fertility rates have declined in all areas and among all groups within China and are now among the lowest found in less developed countries. But how quickly, when, and how far fertility has declined differ among population groups. Fertility has fallen much faster and farther in urban than in rural areas. Urban and rural patterns diverged in the 1960s, as urban rates headed downward throughout the country. Rural rates did not begin to decline until the 1970s and lagged behind urban declines by as much as 10 years in some areas, especially in western provinces. Despite the eventual decline in rural fertility, urban marital fertility has remained 30 percent to 50 percent lower than rural fertility. Rural fertility has remained higher, in part, because the government has allowed many rural families to have a second child.

13.5.13. Policy and Fertility Decline

Socioeconomic factors-including women's education, family income, marriage and childbearing patterns, and women's roles in the family and the labour force-can have a strong influence on fertility. Such factors also affect fertility in China, but the country's strong birth planning programme has tempered some of those socioeconomic influences. China's experience gives demographers a unique opportunity to evaluate the effects of tough policies and birth planning in addition to socioeconomic influences on fertility. There have always been marked regional differences in fertility in China. Before fertility began to decline, regions with higher levels of socioeconomic development had better health and higher fertility. Fertility began to fall earlier in the eastern, more developed provinces.

In the late 1970s, when some of China's biggest fertility declines occurred, less developed regions had higher fertility. Economic development has been associated with fertility declines in many countries, but China is an especially interesting case because it allows researchers to see how the fertility development relationship changed after the onset of a strong government programme to control fertility. As fertility fell, the influence of economic measures on fertility weakened. Early in the decline, income levels had a significant influence on fertility even within provinces. By the mid-1970s, however, individual and community socioeconomic factors had become less important.

Despite the increasing strength of the birth planning program and the weakening effects of socioeconomic factors, there are still significant regional, provincial, and local differences in fertility (and in mortality). Provincial fertility levels have changed markedly over time but have not converged.

Infant mortality has been an especially important indicator of fertility. Chinese counties with low infant mortality rates also had lower fertility. Other socioeconomic indicators were even more strongly linked to fertility in some parts of the country. Community literacy had the greatest effect in the northern and southwestern parts of China while agricultural and industrial output per capita had the strongest effect on fertility levels in eastern and southern China. The resources available for birth planning programmes also play an important role. Programmes may be more effective at lowering fertility in some areas than in others either because they have more resources or use resources more effectively. Wealthier areas have more resources to strengthen their programs by hiring more personnel or providing more attractive incentives for compliance with birth limits. Programmes appear to be more effective in areas with certain socioeconomic characteristics, such as high levels of education.

The wide differences in culture, norms, and fertility preferences among China's heterogeneous population can also affect fertility. Accordingly, birth planning programmes are increasingly being adapted to local needs.

13.5.14. Marriage and Fertility Decline

Marriage has always been a significant institution in China: It establishes or strengthens new political connections, marks the beginning of a new family or (more accurately) a new generation in an existing family, and is recognised as the legitimate start of sexual relations. Marriage has changed profoundly in China in recent years. Not only has women's age at marriage increased, but the timing of marriage in women's lives has also become more concentrated within a narrow age range.

The Chinese government encouraged late marriage as a way to lower fertility and slow population growth. These changes have had a fundamental role in reducing China's fertility, especially in the 1970s and 1980s, since most women in the country have their first birth soon after they marry. By delaying marriage and childbearing, the state has been able to lengthen the gap between generations, lower national fertility, and slow overall population growth.

13.5.15. Assessing China's Policies

China has been able to reduce its fertility and population growth to an extent many did not believe possible. But the country has not met all of its population goals. The difference between the goals and the current situation reflects both the unrealistic nature of some of the goals and the limits to what even a very strong government programme can do to reduce fertility in a short period. There is considerable debate about how much of China's phenomenal fertility decline can be directly attributed to the birth planning policies. Even in a society with a strong government birth control programme, concomitant social and economic changes also influence fertility. The

Chinese government launched a series of effective economic reforms around the time that the most restrictive birth policies took effect.

13.5.16. The 'Missing Girls'

One of the most worrisome effects of the birth planning programme is the "missing girls" phenomenon. Changes in China's sex ratio at birth, or the number of males per 100 females, reveal that millions of girls were "missing" from China's population registers in the early 1980s. These sex ratios have risen to alarming levels, especially for higher-order births.

Four possible explanations of the high sex ratios have received most attention: excess deaths of female babies through infanticide, neglect, or abandonment; underreporting of female births; adoption of female children; and sex-selective abortions. Statistics on these different practices are not available. Even statistics on formal adoption are not easy to obtain, and many adoptions are conducted through unofficial channels. Although officials know that thousands of infant girls are abandoned, they do not know the girls' fate. Recent research suggests that many abandoned infants die and others enter the Chinese welfare system, but many others are adopted by local families. Underreporting of female births-by definition, difficult to measure-is most likely occur in families hoping to hide a birth from authorities, usually so that the couple can try again to have a son.

Female infanticide has been reported in China for centuries, but it is strongly forbidden by law. While it may still be practiced, it is probably relatively rare. Some observers have argued that it would be difficult to get away with such a crime in a society where neighbors and officials are aware of most daily activities. Furthermore, few parents would be able to bear the psychological and moral pain of abandoning or killing a child. One of the most likely causes of the skewed sex ratios at birth is the increasing use of prenatal sex determination and subsequent sexselective abortion. Sex-selective abortion and the underreporting of female births together account for nearly all of the missing girls. Evidence for sexselective abortions is scattered. Parents' ability to determine the sex of a fetus was bolstered by the increasing availability of ultrasound B machines.

13.5.17. Birth Restrictions

Most Chinese accept the state's role in population control, but many disagree with the severe restrictions on the number of children they are allowed to have. The strong desire for sons is central to this resistance: Families who have had a daughter often want to try again for a son. Son preference has a long history in China and is tied to the social and economic roles of males in Chinese families. Family lineage is traced through males, and sons are responsible for caring for their parents in their old age. Marriage practices reflect these traditions. When daughters marry, they leave their birth families to join their husbands' families. In rural areas, few peasants have retirement pensions, so aging parents depend on their children for support. Because daughters have traditionally married out of the family, a couple with no son may end up without financial and personal support. Thus, regardless of their acceptance of the state's control of population growth, most Chinese citizens want at least one son. Many couples would like a daughter as well.

The specter of not having a son has fueled resistance to China's birth planning policies, especially among peasants. This resistance has taken three main routes: confrontation, evasion, and accommodation. Confrontation is often at the local level, where birth planning officials in charge of enforcing birth policies have sometimes been threatened and beaten, their property attacked, and their farm animals killed. More often, women and their families evade restrictions by avoiding birth planning officials, fleeing to another village to avoid discovery, hiding a pregnancy from officials, or discarding birth control methods without the knowledge of officials. Women or their family members sometimes use bribes or other ways to persuade local officials to allow an "unofficial" pregnancy. Local officials often sidestep the rules by underreporting the number of births in their jurisdiction.

Women, their families, and officials have pressured the state to make its policies more flexible, and the government has made some concessions to meet their demands. The official accommodations to the highly valued birth planning policies show how difficult it has been for China to implement a birth planning policy that challenges a strongly patriarchal culture.

13.6. Changing Population of China

China's demographic changes have coincided with fundamental social and economic changes. China is experiencing increasing levels of migration, the growing importance of ethnicity, population aging, environmental degradation, and increasing social and economic inequality. Some of these trends, such as population aging, are largely the result of demographic changes; others, such as issues involving the environment and ethnic identity, are affected by demographic changes; and still others, such as daughters-despite the gender equality guaranteed by the Chinese constitution.

13.6.1. Ethnic Identity in Modern China

Although China is often described as being ethnically homogenous, there is considerable ethnic diversity within the country's borders. China's government recognises 56 official "nationalities"-ethnic groups eligible for special considerations that may include subsidies for certain foods, special consideration on national university exams, more lenient birth planning policies, and other dispensations. These 56 nationalities make up 9 percent of the country's total population, or about 105 million people; the remaining 91 percent are Han Chinese. In addition to these 56 nationalities, however, many more ethnic groups have petitioned for official recognition. Some people want to claim ethnic identity because there are now some advantages to that status, including an allowance for more children. But the greater official acceptance of ethnic diversity in China and an increased interest in ethnic identity throughout the country have also contributed to the rise in ethnic minority affiliation. Many minority groups have increasing contact with counterpart minority communities who live outside China's borders.

China's central government has struggled to balance the advantages of a multiethnic society with the possibility that these groups and their international contacts might pose a threat to Beijing's hold on the nation. People who identify with an ethnic group outside of the country may be less loyal to China, and international contacts make China's borders more porous than the government would prefer. China once projected an image of a united homogenous nation, but these growing minority groups have begun to challenge that picture.

13.6.2. New Trends and Challenges

China experienced dramatic declines in birth and death rates over the past 50 years as the government implemented revolutionary and controversial policies to improve health and slow population growth. With 1.3 billion people, China remains the world's most populous country, but it has lower fertility than the United States and many

European countries. Fewer children, later marriage, and longer life expectancy have affected family structures and created new challenges. The growing proportion of elderly in China is beginning to strain both national and family resources. Lower fertility means that fewer children-and sometimes only one child-will be available to care for elderly family members.

Movement toward a market economy and opening to international trade in the 1990s brought enormous economic growth, but also increased income and health inequalities, encouraged mass labor migration, and exacerbated environ-mental damage. The effects of these dramatic changes on China's fertility, health, economy will ripple through the society for the foreseeable future, and will be felt around the world.

13.7. Future Challenges

In both India and China, the almost universal preference for sons is a major barrier to reducing family size. In cultures where women are subordinate to men and sons contribute more than daughters to families and aging parents, couples may have more children than they would like to ensure they have a son. Some couples in both countries have turned to sex-selective abortions to limit their family size and still have the son they want. While China implements its official policies more effectively than India, deeply entrenched cultural practices and individual preferences thwart both countries' stated goals.

References

Ansley J. Coale, *Rapid Population Change in China, 1952-1982,* Washington, DC: National Academy Press, 1984

Judith Banister, "China: Recent Mortality Levels and Trends", *paper prepared for the annual meeting of the Population Association of America*, Denver, May 1992.

Indian Institute for Population Sciences (IIPS), *India National Family Health Survey, 1992-93*, Bombay, 1995.

Liu Zheng and Li Jianbao, "Characteristics and Priorities of China's Population Control From an International Perspective," *Chinese Journal of Population Science* 5, no. 2, 1993.

Penny Kane, *The Second Billion: Population and Family Planning in China,* Victoria, Australia: Penguin Books, 1987.

CHAPTER 14

Research Methodology in Population Education

14.1. Introduction

Population Education has been defined as an educational process to develop an understanding of inter-relationship between population and development, causes and consequences of population changes, and the criticality of the conditions for population stabilisation. It inculcates among the students rational attitude and responsible behaviour towards population and development issues, so that they make informed decisions. Looking into the objectives of Population Education which aim at influencing the students' attitudes about their present and future population related behaviour and the controversial and inter-disciplinary nature of the subject matter of Population Education,

The teaching method appropriate to Population Education cannot be one in which the teacher rather dictatorially tells students that this behaviour is the right one and all others are wrong. Rather, the ideal teaching method should present and evaluate planable alternatives in terms of the advantages and disadvantages associated with each. And on the basis of this evaluation, a given alternative is either accepted or rejected - with the clear understanding that the right decision for one may be wrong decision for another.

Moreover, the increasingly rapid pace of change implies the need to equip children with the analytical and problem-solving skills to deal with situations as yet undefined and to develop "futuristic - thinking" skills. Realising the importance of such an approach, UNESCO's report 'Learning: Treasure Within' observes:

'The teacher's wok is not confined simply to transmitting information or even knowledge, it also entails presenting that knowledge in the form of a statement of problems within a certain context and putting the problems into perspective, so that the learner can link their solution to broader issues. It is becoming increasingly necessary in modem societies for teaching to help form individual judgement and a sense of individual responsibility so as to enable pupils to develop the ability to foresee changes and to adjust to them, in other words to continue learning throughout their lives. It is through working under and through dialogue with, the teacher that a pupils' critical faculty is helped to develop.'

A learner centered model aiming at participation and learning by doing rather than the traditional teacher-centered model is to be adopted in teaching of Population Education as has been emphasised in the the report 'Learning Without Burden'. A Participatory Student-centered Model for teaching of Population Education covering substance, procedures and the classroom environment is presented below:

14.2. Participatory Student-centred Model

The Participatory model as depicted above, emphasises inquiry skills which are actually competencies required for exploring social reality. Hence, Inquiry is considered to be the basic methodology of Population Education.

14.2.1. Inquiry Approach

The term 'Inquiry Approach' has been used interchangeably with such terms as "Discovery approach", "Problem-solving", "Independent learning/teaching", "Inductive method", "Deductive method", "Conceptual approach", "Process approach", "Socratic questioning", "Investigation" and "Value Clarification". Emphasis in all these approaches is on learner's thinking and finding, although the steps followed may be different. Hence, the Inquiry approach should be looked at as a total environment or orientation of teaching and learning. As a teaching style, in the Inquiry approach, the learner tries to find out, to learn more or to better understand some aspect of social reality.

14.2.2. Procedures

Recognising and stating the problem: The topic 'Effects of Population Growth to Socio-economic Development' is to be approached by the students as a problem by presenting/discussing, conflicting views on the issue i.e. whether population growth has a positive or negative impact on socioeconomic development. The statement of the problem should be explicit, precise and researchable. Population growth is to be taken as independent variable and socioeconomic development as dependent variable.

Formulating the hypothesis: A hypothesis is to be arrived at through the process of elimination of tentative answers to the problem on the basis of discussions. At this stage, a refinement of the statement of the problem is to be made.

Data Gathering: To provide in-depth discussion of the tentative answers, the elated data is to be gathered. Data may be gathered through observation, interview, questionnaire, case studies, documentary analysis etc. For testing the above hypotheses, documentary analysis seem to be a suitable device for data gathering. Two sets of data from a relevant document are to be gathered providing evidences that the countries having planned population growth have a high rate of socioeconomic development and the countries having a population growth rate of 2 percent or above, have a very low rate of socioeconomic development. The relevant document here may be UNDP's Human Development Report, 1998.

Applying the Conclusions/Generalisations: By going through the above process, the students may think of making socioeconomic development as independent variable and population growth a dependent one thereby may formulate a new hypotheses "High rate of socio-economic development tends to bring about a decline in the population growth rate".

14.2.3. Value Clarification

In teaching of population education, three main affective objectives are to be achieved: involvement, concern and response. Through the process of involvement - involvement in issues and problems and involvement with others, a person develops a feeling of concern, which may lead to the possibilities of incorporating the same with his system of values. Value may be defined as a conception or standard, cultural or merely personal, by which things are compared and approved or disapproved relative to one another - held to be relatively desirable or undesirable, more meritorious or less, more correct or less. All kinds of "things" may be evaluated: feelings, ideas, actions, qualities, objects, persons, groups, means.

Values tend to change very slowly, in response to a number of influences. Education can help facilitate this process by helping learners understand their own values, and those of others' that may be in conflict with these. There is general agreement within the field of population education that value clarification is a necessary, and indeed, perhaps the most important aspect of learners' preparation for choice and decision making. Value Clarification is a process of inquiry and examination, which is intended to strengthen (or awaken) learners' conscious allegiance to the fundamental core values, which bind the society and the nation; and to develop in learners a readiness to examine values in future choice and decision-making.

14.3. Evaluation in Population Education

Education and evaluation are inter-related processes. Evaluation is as old as the process of education itself. Education in its wider sense implies not only acquisition of knowledge, but also development of abilities, skills, personality qualities, which are important in individual's personal and social life. The function of evaluation in education is to provide a systematic assessment of the development of these qualities as an outcome of educational endeavour. Since population education is also an educational process aiming at inculcating rational attitude and responsible behaviour among the learners towards population and development issues and helping them to take informed decisions, role of evaluation is of utmost importance. Without the benefit of evaluation, one is unable to determine how well the programme has achieved its goal. Evaluation also serves as the basis for the improvement of the way activities are carried out. Evaluation is also an effort at discovering whether certain activities have led to desired effects or outcomes.

Evaluation in education means describing something, in terms of selected attributes and judging the degree of acceptability or suitability of that which has been described. The something which is described can be any aspect of the educational scene.

In broadest sense, the term evaluation is defined as a systematic assessment of the value or worth of 'something'. This 'something' could be a programme or a segment of a programme, a technique or strategy used, educational materials or a situation prevalent in a particular community. It is also defined as the collection and use of information to make decisions about an educational programme like population education programme. Principles of evaluation in population education are essentially principles of evaluation in education. It is true that evaluation in population education is difficult because population education aims at effecting behavioural changes in the affective domain to a greater degree. It has cognitive component only to the extent that is needed to bring attitudinal changes.

Effort, effect, adequacy, efficiency and process are the five major aspects that must be assessed in order to ascertain success or failure of population education programme. When programme implementers evaluate effort, they try to measure the quantity as well as the quality of available resources. This type of evaluation is called input evaluation. It involves taking of all available resources, both human and material (personnel, money, educational tools, methods or techniques), and of the activities generated by these resources. The number of qualified personnel, logistics required for programme operation, the number of educational materials distributed to the target audience the kind and number of activities conducted, etc. are some of the features considered in input evaluation.

In evaluating effect, the main concern is to measure the results or the outcomes of the efforts made in terms of intended objectives. In other words, programme evaluators want to know the extent to which their objectives have been achieved. This type of evaluation is referred to as impact or outcome evaluation.

In evaluating adequacy, the effectiveness of the programme in relation to the population, it is intended to serve, is determined. This type of evaluation is otherwise known as potency effectiveness. An index of adequacy can be computed by multiplying the rate of effectiveness of the number of people exposed to the programme. The rate of effectiveness is defined as the proportion of the target population that has been reached by the programme. For example, if a population education programme operating in a particular school reaches 100 out of a total of 1000 school children, the rate of effectiveness of the programme is 10 per cent. In as much as only 100 students were covered, the programme effect or impact will actually be felt by only 10 per cent. To make the index meaningful, it should be compared with a pre-determined level of satisfaction.

In evaluating efficiency, programme administrators make a cost-benefit or cost effectiveness analysis whenever possible. They study the benefits derived from the educational activity in relation to the costing of all programme activities. It is called realised effectiveness. In process evaluation, the evaluator is interested to know how and why a programme works or does not work, or how the different programme inputs can be used to arrive at desired results.

14.3.1. Types of Evaluation

Evaluation is a continuous process, which can begin even before the initiation of a programme and has no end as long as the programme is in existence. Evaluation can be of the following types:

14.3.1.1. Pre-programme evaluation

Pre-programme evaluation provides base line information on knowledge, attitudes, skills, etc. of the learner. Such evaluation provides information on what are the needs of learners, what are their strengths and weaknesses. In population education, it tells the implementers the areas to be emphasised and the areas not to be emphasised.

14.3.1.2. In-programme or formative evaluation

Basic purpose of evaluation here is to identify the strengths and weaknesses of the programme during the process of implementation and to suggest ways and means of improving the strengths and reducing its weaknesses through the use of appropriate strategies. In formative evaluation various aspects of population education programme like curriculum and materials, teaching-learning process, teacher training, programme management or programme effects can be evaluated.

14.3.1.3. Post-programme or summative evaluation

It is the evaluation of the outcome of a programme both on a short-term and on a long-term basis. Post evaluation determines whether programme objectives have been achieved, and whether learners have measurable gains in knowledge, attitude and skills.

Formative evaluation aims at evaluating inputs, effectiveness, and process whereas summative evaluation or post-programme evaluation aims at evaluating the outcome, impact or effectiveness at the end of the programme.

14.3.1.4. Substantive aspects of evaluation

The problem focused and future oriented nature of population education programme makes it necessary to focus its evaluation on higher level cognitive in addition to the simple recall and interpretation of population concepts and statistics.

Different levels of evaluation are inter-linked with each other. For example, the awareness of a particular feature of adolescence education such as the problem of HIV/AIDS is related with the level of concern or commitment to improve the situation. A deeper understanding of the modes of transmission, consequences of HIV/AIDS infection and of creation of awareness and formation of attitude for prevention occur simultaneously. At the same time, students and teachers need to acquire abilities to plan and implement instructions to attain the objectives. In such situation both cognitive and affective aspects as well as teaching skills should be evaluated in an integrated manner.

14.3.2. Planning Evaluation

For planning evaluation activity, the following aspects should be taken into consideration:

14.3.2.1. Identification of programme goals and objectives

The first step in the evaluation process is the identification of programme goals and objectives. Very often, one finds it difficult to make evaluation of any teaching endeavour simply because one does not know what the teaching activity is intended for. Sometimes, programmes are formulated and implemented without definite and specific objectives. Teaching techniques are selected and used without thinking of what they are supposed to achieve.

The programme objectives to be evaluated must, therefore, be stated in behavioural terms. By evaluation, the changes that have taken place in behaviour will be ascertained.

14.3.2.2. Examine programme activities and implementation procedures

It is imperative to know not only the programme objectives or activity specific objectives but also the activities and the manner of execution of these activities to help the learners to achieve the programme objectives. Evaluation is not confined to the assessment of the results of the teaching learning activities, it also involves an examination of the means adopted to reach the end.

14.3.2.3. Indicators of evaluation

One of the most critical tasks of an evaluator of population education programmes is to determine the indicators. An indicator is a measure to judge the performance and or effectiveness of the programme. To do so, the indicator must have a reference point or objective against which the measures can be judged. Some of the indicators can be of quantitative nature like the number of lessons included, number of materials produced, number of teachers and other functionaries trained. Some indicators are related to the measure of knowledge, attitudes and to the behaviour of learners. These indicators help determine the extent of change taken place in learners' knowledge, attitude skills, understanding, values, beliefs, habits and practices as a result of the programme activities. These are measures according to the major themes identified in population education.

14.3.2.4. Standard techniques/instruments of evaluation

After defining the objectives of evaluation, the next step is to determine the standard techniques and types of instruments with the help of which one can reveal whether programme objectives have been achieved. Students - teachers will learn more if evaluation is made systematic and specific through the use of standardised forms and instruments.

14.3.2.5. Self administered questionnaire

The questionnaire is perhaps the most commonly used instrument in data collection. Questionnaire often takes the form of a self-administered instrument that is given to students to fill up. It is also possible that the same instrument is sent by mail. The questinnaire is useful in dealing with relatively straightforward items, especially those answerable with a 'yes', 'no' or multiple choice items.

14.3.2.6. Structured or unstructured interview schedules

In sensitive topics such as those dealing with personal or family matters, it is better to collect data through interviews. Interview schedule may also be used where the researchers can probe, repeat or modify the questions to adjust to situation. The interview schedule can be structured if the interviewer follows a specific set of questions that are listed in the schedule. It is called unstructured when the interviewer follows no set questions and maintains flexibility and openers in the wording and flow of questions. To maintain a fruitful interview, the researcher must be a very good listener and willing to make adjustment in terms of both content and pace.

14.3.2.7. Interpretative exercise

An interpretative exercise consists of a series of objective type items based on a common set of data. Factual data presented in the form of charts, maps graphs and case studies can be used. This type of interpretative exercise can be used to assess the ability of the learner to interpret and analyse age structure, dependency ratio, school age population, etc.

14.3.2.8. Data collection

The next step in the evaluation process is the collection of desired information. In the collection of data, there are two important things - the sources of information and the method of collecting the data. Sources of data can be primary or secondary. Primary sources include the original documents i.e. the first reporting of facts while secondary sources are facts from primary sources.

The data collection methods include sampling and data collection techniques. Sampling refers to the gathering of information from a representative population instead of the whole population under study. There are a number of ways through which a representative sample can be obtained. These are simple random sampling, stratified random sampling, systematic - random sampling cluster, multi-stage and purposive sampling, etc. The size of the sample depends on many things such as the nature of the analysis to be performed, the desired precision, the number of variables and the availability of funds. After the identification of the sample size, one or more instruments discussed can be made use of depending upon the objectives of the evaluation.

14.3.2.9. Analysis and interpretation

The last step in the evaluation process is the analysis and interpretation of data collected. For meaningful interpretation, mass data need to be reduced to meaningful number by using various statistical devices like averages, mean, percentage, correlation regression etc. For materials evaluation, relevance, suitability for age, needs of learners and sequencing are also to be seen.

14.3.2.10. Problems related to evaluation

The term evaluation is misunderstood many times - Some people avoid their project being evaluated as they consider evaluation as a fault-finding exercise.

14.3.2.11. Problem of identification of objectives

One of the difficulties, which the evaluators are facing, is regarding objectives of population education. Different people perceive different objectives and some times there is no agreement. Another problem associated with these objectives is that the behavioural results of these objectives are not immediately evident. Evaluation of behaviour, thus requires extended follow-up and time series studies.

In population education the most common indicators used are knowledge and attitude as the available proxy for behaviour. However, researchers have shown quite a low correlation of knowledge and attitude with behaviour.

14.3.2.12. Problem of evaluation design and instrument

There are certain technical problems associated with evaluation such as sampling, standardised instruments for measuring knowledge, attitudes and decisions, data-analysis. Evaluation results can be better if controlled group design is used. But it is very difficult to conduct evaluation in population education with controlled experiments as there are many extraneous factors working in the community, which are beyond any control. One, therefore, cannot know to what extent the changing indices represent successful or unsuccessful programme activities.

In Population Education, the ultimate measure of effectiveness is behaviour. There is need to have better instruments and predictor of future behaviour. A combination of conventional techniques and situational techniques may help in yielding better results.

References

Jangira N.K., *Teacher training and teacher effectiveness an experiment in teachers behaviour,* National Publishing House, Delhi, 1991.

Pandey, J.L. and Jain, D.P., *Syllabus on population education for plus two stage,* New Delhi: NCERT, 1987.

Sike O.J., *Population education – An article published in international encyclopedia of population vol. I,* New York : 1992

Sirageldin, Ismail and others, *Evaluating population programmes,* New York: St. Martin's Press, 1983.

Unesco, *Preparing teachers for Population Education – A handbook*, Paris : UNESCO, 1983.

Unesco, *Teaching methodologies for population education – Inquiry/ discovery, value clarification,* Bangkok: UNESCO Regional Office for Education in Asia and the Pacific, 1986.

Unesco, *Manual on evaluation in population education,* UNESCO, Bangkok: Thailand 1979.

UNFPA, "Framework of selected indicators for evaluating the impact of population education programmes", *Technical report,* Number 33, 1996.

Unesco, *Teaching Methodologies for Population Education: Inquiry/Discovery Approach; values clarification*, ROEAP, Bangkok 1985.

Unesco, *Evaluative research in population education: Manual arising out of a regional training workshop,* Manila, 20-31 May 1985.

Unesco, "Educator training for out of school population", *A practical guide,* Unesco Bangkok: May 1984.

Villanueva, C.L., *On the effectiveness of the discovery approach teaching method for population education,* Phillipines: Information & Research Utilization Division Population Center Foundation, 1976.

Bibliography

Ansley J. Coale, *Rapid Population Change in China, 1952-1982,* Washington, DC: National Academy Press, 1984

Bain, I., "Southeast Asia, International Migration, Quarterly Review", *special edition on Migration and HIV/AIDS*, Vol 36:4, 1998.

Berryman, A. A., *Principles of population dynamics and their application*, Cheltenham, UK: Stanley Thornes, 1999.

Caldwell, John C., "Toward a Restatement of Demographic Transition Theory", *Population and Development Review* 2: 321-66, 1976.

.........., "Mass education as a determinant of the timing of fertility decline", *Population and Development Review*, New York (June), 1980.

Caouette, T et al., "Assessment of Reproductive and Sexual Health", *Concerns and Realities of Migrant Workers in Burma and Thailand (Draft),* Institute for Population and Social Science Research, Mahidol University, Thailand, 1999.

Cassen, Robert and Contributors, "Population and Development", Old Debates, New Conclusions. Washington DC: Overseas Development Council. 1994

Colin Clark, "Population Growth and Land Use", 2nd ed. *an analysis of specific problems*, 1977.

Cromartie, Michael (e.d.), *The Nine Lives of Population Control*, Grand Rapids (MI): Ethics and Public Policy Center and Wm. B. Eerdmans Publishing Co. 1995.

Cruz Leonardo de la, *Population education: Nature, goal and role,* Bangkok: UNESCO, 1978.

Dasmann, Raymond F., "Environmental Conservation", 5th ed., *a study of the human influence on nature and its consequences for human population*, 1984

Eberstadt, Nicholas, "The Population Implosion," in *The Wall Street Journal*, Thursday October 16, 1997.

Ehsanul Haq, *Sociology of Population in India*, Macmillan India, 2007

Elwell, Frank W., "A Commentary on Malthus's 1798", *Essay on Population as Social Theory*, The Edwin Mellon Press, 2001.

Eric B. Ross, *The Malthus factor: population, poverty, and politics in capitalist development*, Zed Books, London. ISBN 1-85649-564-7, 1998.

Family Health International, "Making Prevention Work: No.10. Crossing Borders - Reaching Mobile Population at Risk", May, 1999.

Fernandez I., "Migration and HIV/AIDS", *In: 4th International Congress on AIDS in Asia and the Pacific in Manila*, October 1997.

Fitzenberger, B., et al., "The gender gap in labor market participation and employment: A cohort analysis for West Germany" *Journal of Population Economics,* 17, No. 1 (2004): 83-116.

Geust, P., "Overview of the Population Mobility Situation in Asia and its Implications for HIV/AIDS", *paper presented at the Fifth International Congress on AIDS in Asia and the Pacific*, Kuala Lumpur, 20-27 October, 1999.

Grover R.P., and Ramesh Kumar Bhardwaj, *Population Education in India*, Ambala Cantt, The Associated Publishers, 2002.

Hartmann, Betsy, *Reproductive Rights & Wrongs: The Global Policies of Population Control*, Boston: South End Press 1995.

Hollander, Samuel, *The Economics of Thomas Robert Malthus*, University of Toronto Press, 1997.

Hsu, L.-N. and J. d. Guerny, "Population Movement, Development and HIV/AIDS: Looking Towards the Future", Bangkok, *UNDP & FAO*, 2000.

Hutabarat, Sans S., et al., *Population education in Indonesia,* Jakarta: National Family Planning Coordination Board, 1979.

Indian Institute for Population Sciences (IIPS), *India National Family Health Survey, 1992-93*, Bombay, 1995.

Jacobson, Willard J., *Population education: A knowledge base,* New York: Teachers College, Columbia University, 1979.

James, Patricia, *Population Malthus : his Life and Times*, Londen : Routledge and Kegan Paul, 1979.

Jangira N.K., *Teacher training and teacher effectiveness an experiment in teachers behaviour,* National Publishing House, Delhi, 1991.

Jayasuriya, J.E., *Curriculum innovation through population education,* Colombo: Associated Educational Publishers, 1978.

Joseph Raju B., Gadde Annie Anitha and Digumarti Bhaskara Rao, *Population Education*, New Delhi, Sonali, 2004.

Judith Banister, "China: Recent Mortality Levels and Trends", *paper prepared for the annual meeting of the Population Association of America*, Denver, May 1992.

Kaldor, J. et al., ed., "HIV surveillance in hard-to-reach populations", *AIDS* 15 (Suppl. 3), April 2001.

Kasun, Jacqueline, *The War Against Population*, San Francisco: Ignatius Press 1988.

Kelly P., "Managing HIV Vulnerability of Mobile Populations: Methodologies for Data Collection", *In: Satellite Symposium, 4th International Congress on AIDS in Asia and the Pacific in Manila.* October 1997

Kerrigan, D., *Peer Education and HIV/AIDS: Concepts, Uses and Challenges,* Washington, DC: HORIZONS/Population Council, 1999

Keyfitz Nathan (ed.), *Population and Biology: Bridge Between Disciplines*, a collection of papers on biological aspects of demography, 1984.

Klemola, T., Korpimaki, E. & Koivula, M., "Rate of population change in voles from different phases of the population cycle", *Oikos,* 2002

Kline, David and David Harman ed., *Issues in population education*, Lexington, Mass: Lexington Books, 1976.

Krebs, C. J., *Two paradigms of population regulation, Wildl. Res.* 22, 1–10, 1995

Kumarasena Harsha, *A Textbook of Population Education*, New Delhi, Dominant, 2004.

Kuzynski, Robert R., *The Measurement of Population Growth*, Gordon and Breach Science Publishers, New York, 1969.

Lakshmi Narasaiah M., *Population and Education*, New Delhi, Discovery Publishing House, 2007.

Lamptey, P., "Reducing heterosexual transmission of HIV in poor countries", *British Medical Journal,* 324:207–211 2002.

Larry Hobbs, "Complexity of factors involved in human population growth", *Environmental Health Perspectives*, Sept 2004.

Liu Zheng and Li Jianbao, "Characteristics and Priorities of China's Population Control From an International Perspective," *Chinese Journal of Population Science* 5, no. 2, 1993.

Livi-Bacci, Massimo, *Population and Nutrition: An Essay on European Demographic History,* Cambridge: Cambridge University Press, 1991.

Lutz, W. & Qiang, R., "Determinants of human population growth", *Phil. Trans. R. Soc. Lond.* B 357,1197–1210, 2002.

Lutz, W., Sanderson, W. & Scherbov, S., "The end of world population growth", *Nature,* 2001.

Malthus, T. R., *An essay on the principle of population*, London: J. Johnson, 1798

McArdle, Nancy with Jan Erik Hall and Peter Zlotnick, "Population and Employment Decentralization Trends as of 1986", Joint Center for Housing Studies of Harvard University. Working Paper W88-2. Cambridge, MA. 1988.

McKeown, Thomas, *The Origins of Human Disease,* Oxford: Basil Blackwell, 1988.

Murdoch, W.W., "Population regulation in theory and practice", *Ecology* 75, 271–287, 1994

NCERT, *Population education; A draft syllabus, (Mimeograph)*, New Delhi, NCERT, 1971.

........., *Minimum essential contents of population education*, (Mimeograph), New Delhi: NCERT, 1987.

........., *National seminar on population education,* New Delhi: NCERT, 1969.

Nguyen T H., *Population Redistribution Policy and Migration Trends in Vietnam: Past, Present and Future*, 1998.

O.J., *Population education*, *International encyclopedia of population,* Volume One, New York: the Free Press, 1984.

Pandey, J.L. and Jain, D.P., *Syllabus on population education for plus two stage,* New Delhi: NCERT, 1987.

Penny Kane, *The Second Billion: Population and Family Planning in China,* Victoria, Australia: Penguin Books, 1987.

Prah Ruger J., "Combating HIV/AIDS in developing countries", *British Medical Journal,* 2004.

Pritchett, Lant H., "Desired Fertility and the Impact of Population Policies," in *Population and Development Review*, Vol.20 (no.1), March 1994.

Puhani, P.A., "Poland on the dole: The effect of reducing the unemployment benefit entitlement period during transition" *Journal of Population Economics,* Vol. 13, No. 1, 35-44, 2000.

Rajesh, *Population and Development Education in Indian Universities*, Delhi, Indian Publihers, 2004.

Roed, K. and M. Nordberg, "Have the relative employment prospects for the low-skilled deteriorated after all?" *Journal of Population Economics*, 17, No. 1, 2004.

Salmony S.E., "Food and population growth", *Environmental Health Perspectives,* 112:A339-A340, 2004.

Shakoori Batool, "Demographic transition and its Implicaitons on Demgraphic Tranisition and its Implications on Employment and International Migration", *Fourth Coordination Meeting on Internatinal Migration,* Population Division Department of Economic and Social Affairs United Nations Secretariat, New York, 26-27 October 2005.

Sharma, R.C., *Population resources, environment and quality of life,* Delhi: Dhanpat Rai & Sons, 1988.

Sheshadri, C. and J.L. Pandey, *Population education: A national source book*, New Delhi: NCERT, 1991.

Shlomo Avineri, *The Social and Political Thought of Karl Marx*, Cambridge University Press, 1968.

Sike O.J., *Population education – An article published in international encyclopedia of population vol. I,* New York : 1992

.........., "Reconceptualization of population education", *Technical Paper,* Number 2, UNFPA, New York: 1993.

Simon, Julian L., *Population Matters*, New Brunswick (NJ): Transaction Publishers, 1990.

........., *Population and Development in Poor Countries*, Princeton: Princeton University Press. 1992

Sirageldin, Ismail and others, *Evaluating population programmes,* New York: St. Martin's Press, 1983.

Skeldon R., "Population Mobility and HIV Vulnerability in South East Asia: An Assessment and Analysis", *UNDP Southeast Asia HIV and Development Project*, February, 2000.

Spencer, Herbert, *First Principles*, New York: D. Appleton and Company, 1897.

Tilottama Senapati, *Curriculum Development in Population Education*, New Delhi, Anmol Publishers, 2006.

UNAIDS, "Migration and AIDS", *International Migration*, Vol. 36 (4): 445-468, 1998.

UNAIDS, "Migration and HIV/AIDS", *Program Coordination Board Second Ad hoc Thematic Meeting*, New Delhi, December, 1998.

UNDP, "Reduction of HIV Vulnerability within the Land Transport Sector", *UNDP-SEA HIV Development Project*, 2000.

Unesco, "Educator training for out of school population", *A practical guide,* Unesco Bangkok: May 1984.

........., "Future directions of population education", *Report of a Regional Consultative Seminar*, Manila, 14-21 August 1978.

........., "Population education: A contemporary concern", *ISCOMPE Education Studies Documents* No. 28, Paris: UNESCO, 1978.

........., "Population education: innovative structures and approaches", *Report of a Regional Workshop*, New Delhi, 23-29 October 1979.

........., *Evaluative research in population education: Manual arising out of a regional training workshop,* Manila, 20-31 May 1985.

........., *Manual on evaluation in population education,* UNESCO, Bangkok: Thailand 1979.

........., Regional Office for Education in Asia and the Pacific, "Problems and strategies for curriculum development in population education", *A paper presented to the Group Training course in Population Education*, Bangkok: 14 July to 15 August 1975.

........., Teaching methodologies for population education – Inquiry/discovery, value clarification, Bangkok: UNESCO Regional Office for Education in Asia and the Pacific, 1986.

UNFPA, "Framework of selected indicators for evaluating the impact of population education programmes", *Technical report,* Number 33, 1996.

........., "Programme of action", *adopted at the International Conference on Population and Development*, Cairo, New York: UNFPA, 5-13 September 1994.

UNICEF, "Mobile Populations and HIV Vulnerability: Approaches to Applied Research", Bangkok, UNICEF, UNAIDS, 1998.

Valkonen, T., "Differentials and trends in life expectancy by gender and occupational class: measurement and explanations", *Paper presented at the seminar on health and other welfare differences between population groups*, Helsinki, 13 and 14 March 2000.

Venkataiah S., *Population Education,* New Delhi, Anmol, 2001.

Villanueva, C.L., *On the effectiveness of the discovery approach teaching method for population education,* Phillipines: Information & Research Utilization Division Population Center Foundation, 1976.

Weinhold B., "Infectious disease: the human cost of our environmental errors, *Environmental Health Perspectives*, 112:A32-A39, 2004.

Winkleby, M. A., and others, "Socioeconomic status and health: how education, income and occupation contribute to risk factors for cardiovascular disease", *American Journal of Public Health*, Washington, D.C.

World Bank, "Priorities and Strategies for Education", *A World Bank Review*, Washington, D.C.: World Bank, 1995.